Arguments for Socialism

Series editor: John Harrison

Arguments for Socialism is a series of popular and provocative
books which deal with the economic and political crisis in Britain
today. The series argues the need for a radical rethinking of major
political questions and contributes to the debates on
strategy for the left.

'One of the main reasons why the Tories swept to power in 1979 was
that the Labour movement had over the years almost ceased to argue
for socialism. This series, *Arguments for Socialism*, can play a
significant part in re-establishing the necessity for a socialism that is
democratic, libertarian and humane.' *Tony Benn*

Blowing the Whistle

The Politics of Sport

Garry Whannel

Pluto Press

First published in 1983 by Pluto Press Limited,
The Works, 105a Torriano Avenue,
London NW5 2RX

British Library Cataloguing in Publication Data
Whannel, Garry   Blowing the whistle.—(Arguments for socialism)
1. Sports—Political aspects
I. Title
306'.483   GV181.3
ISBN 0-86104-508-4

Cover designed by Clive Challis A Gr R
Cover photograph: All Sport/Adrian Murrell
Computerset by Promenade Graphics Limited
Block 23a Lansdown Industrial Estate, Cheltenham GL51 8PL
Printed and bound in Great Britain
by Richard Clay (The Chaucer Press) Limited, Bungay, Suffolk

Contents

To Paddy

Acknowledgements

Writing this book has been very hard work, and I am glad it is over. I have tried to avoid offering easy answers and over-simple conclusions. I hope that socialists will become more active in debate and struggle about the organisation of sport and leisure. All books depend heavily upon hidden labour and I would like to thank John Harrison, Richard Kuper and the staff at Pluto Press and at the various libraries I haunt. In particular I am grateful to Michele Shoebridge at the Sport Documentation Centre, and Neil Somerville at the BBC Written Archives Centre.

Although this book is in a sense mine, I can claim no monopoly of ownership of the ideas within it. I owe a great debt to the writers mentioned in the booklist, whose work I have liberally plundered. As important, though, has been a long series of conversations and arguments, some fleeting and casual, some regular and intense, and for this I would like to thank Alan Lovell, Phil Shaw, Susan Boyd-Bowman, Colin Sparks, John Clarke, Dorothy Hobson, Richard Collins, Chas Critcher, Gabrielle Bown, Stuart Hall, Edward Buscombe, Angela McRobbie, Alan Tomlinson, Terry Lovell, Richard Johnson, Stuart Cosgrove, and Toni Williamson. Above all, the continued enthusiasm of Nicky North, Michael O'Shaughnessy and Michael Jackson for the project has left me at times baffled but always highly grateful. Thank you.

1.

Politics on the Pitch

The 1980 Moscow Olympics were the occasion of an enthralling battle, fought out between the stadium and the television screen. At stake was the interpretation of the games. The Soviet Union controlled the pictures, British television commanded the microphone.

The Soviet Union started impressively with a huge mosaic of people holding coloured cards that spelled the message 'Sport, you are peace'. David Coleman, playing for the BBC, countered by referring to the human mosaic, 'so popular in communist countries'. At home we wondered if he had ever watched BBC's *Match of the Day*, which used to kick off with a similar mosaic revealing the inspiring sight of Jimmy Hill.

The Soviet Union then undermined its early advantage with the bizarre sight of a phalanx of men goosestepping along, right arms aloft clutching doves. Few images so perfectly captured the ambiguities of the Olympic movement.

The battle raged on through the games. British television constantly reminded us that 'our' team was competing under the Olympic flag, while Russian cameras zoomed in on hordes of 'unofficial' Union Jacks in the crowd.

Lord Killanin, head of the International Olympic Committee, made a dramatic late appearance in the closing ceremony to ask sportspeople of the world to unite in peace before a holocaust descended. The great mosaic produced an image of the Moscow mascot crying in sadness at the closing of the games. Coleman countered brilliantly: 'Mika the mascot sheds a cardboard tear – so this is, perhaps, a moment to remember the real grief called for elsewhere which has led to half the world staying away.' It is hard to believe that anyone will ever be able to say again, with a straight face, that sport is nothing to do with politics.

Yet 'Keep politics out of sport' has been the traditional cry of sports leaders, journalists and politicians. Any attempt to raise questions about sport and the society in which it is played is habitually derided. This criticism, levelled with monotonous regularity at the anti-apartheid movement, enables the sport and political establishments to preserve the image of sport as a nice cosy ghetto, insulated from the rest of the social world.

So it came as a shock to many when 1980 began with strident calls for a sporting boycott from the establishment. In the closing week of 1979 Soviet troops had poured into Afghanistan to buttress the crumbling government. President Carter and Prime Minister Thatcher responded by calling on western nations to boycott the forthcoming Olympics.

Overnight people who for years had been insisting that politics be kept out of sport began shaking their heads and saying that unfortunately you cannot keep politics out of sport. It was a dramatic U-turn.

Six months of drama and farce followed. In January the International Olympic Committee refused to move the games from Moscow and in February the Sports Council and the Central Council for Physical Recreation opposed the boycott. But a United States boycott looked more likely.

In March 78 British athletes said they would go even if the British Olympic Association pulled out. But the BOA soon confirmed that it would go to Moscow.

The government stepped up its pressure. In a petty and vindictive move it instructed civil service departments not to award special leave to Moscow-bound athletes. In April top British shotputter Geoff Capes, refused time off for Moscow, resigned from the police force.

Pressure seemed to hit the television plans. Cliff Morgan, head of BBC Outside Broadcasts, announced that coverage of the games would be as normal. The following day the board of governors issued a statement saying that there would not be full coverage. Both BBC and ITV slashed planned coverage by 75 per cent. The forty-odd hours screened by each channel were almost entirely outside peak viewing time.

In retrospect the Carter–Thatcher boycott attempt was a dismal failure. It alienated public opinion whilst having no discernible effect on Soviet policy towards Afghanistan. The games were a great triumph despite the absent countries. British athletes were conspicuously successful.

The boycott campaign was actually less of an about-face by the establishment than is often supposed. Many people had suggested a boycott of Moscow long before Afghanistan, not least British Foreign Secretary David Owen in 1978. A boycott campaign supported by Tory MPs and members of the National Association for Freedom had been active from the start of 1979.

The idea had been floated within the sport world too. Sports Council member Laddie Lucus suggested a Moscow boycott two years before the Olympics, in protest at the treatment of Jewish dissidents. The proposal was discussed by the Sports Council, which decided it was a matter for the British Olympic Association.

Government attempts to use sport to further foreign policy are nothing new. From its modern revival in 1896 the Olympic movement has often been the site of international wrangles and power politics.

The Olympic Game

The first modern Olympic Games were held in Athens in 1896. They were a somewhat disorganised affair. But the potential of international competition was evident and the movement was under way. Links with international capitalism were soon apparent in the connections between the 1900 games and the Paris Universal Exhibition, and the 1904 games, held alongside the St Louis World Fair.

Business interests were again apparent in the 1908 London Olympics. Britain, who had just signed a trade agreement with the Russians, tried to insist that Finland march behind the Russian flag, a demand the Finns resisted. The American team refused to dip their flag in homage to the British king.

In 1912 in Stockholm competitors could no longer enter as individuals but only as part of a national team, and the Finns had to compete under the Russian flag. After war prevented the 1916 games the defeated nations – Germany, Austria, Hungary, Bulgaria and Turkey – were barred in 1920 and so, in the wake of the communist revolution, was the Soviet Union.

The Amsterdam Games of 1928 included women's athletic events for the first time. But the sight of exhausted women in the 800 metres so upset the men of the IOC that they refused to allow women to run the distance again. This absurd ban lasted until 1964.

The Berlin Games of 1936 are notorious for their Nazi pageantry. A strong campaign in America to boycott the games in protest at the vicious suppression of the Jews was foiled when the American representative was expelled from the IOC. But Hitler's attempt to use the games to celebrate Aryan superiority was beautifully undermined. Black American athlete Jesse Owens won four gold medals, breaking the Olympic Record each time. Hitler stalked out in disgust.

The first post-war games were held in London in 1948. Once again the defeated nations – Germany, Italy and Japan – were not invited. Up until 1952 military men could enter only if they were commissioned officers, but from this date the privilege was extended to sergeants. Corporals and privates remained barred.

In 1956 five nations – Iraq, Netherlands, Lebanon, Egypt and Spain – withdrew in protest at the British and French invasion of Suez. Following the Soviet invasion of Hungary, tension was high and there were violent incidents in a water-polo match between the Soviet Union and Hungary, and in a football match between the Soviet Union and Yugoslavia.

In 1964 South Africa was suspended for practising apartheid in sport and persistently selecting all-white teams. It was finally expelled from the Olympic movement in 1970.

In 1972 the rebel regime in Rhodesia was barred. In 1976 20 African nations withdrew in protest at New Zealand's tour of South Africa. Taiwan also withdrew after the Canadian government refused to allow it to compete as 'The Republic of China'.

Sport has always been an integral part of international diplomacy. When the United States first began to reopen relations with China in the 1970s the first sign of a thaw was the arrangement of a table tennis match. This gambit became known as ping-pong diplomacy. I can never hear the phrase 'shuttle diplomacy' without imagining Kissinger umpiring a nightmare badminton match between Sadat and Begin.

Outside the stadium

Governments use major sporting events to present a national image on the world stage. So those who stage Olympics and World Cups become determined not to allow the appearance of dissent to mar their public relations.

When the 1968 Olympics were allocated to Mexico the student movement mounted a campaign to protest at the cost of the games, a huge financial burden on a poor country. Shortly before the games began the army opened fire on a demonstration, killing 260 and injuring 1,000.

The allocation of the 1978 World Cup to Argentina strengthened the resolve of the junta to present an acceptable image to the world. During the years leading up to 1978 an estimated 15,000 people disappeared, believed killed by the security forces.

In the months leading up to the Moscow Olympics drunks, hooligans and dissidents were rounded up and headed out of Moscow. They were allowed back only after the tourists had departed.

In 1982, during the Commonwealth Games in Brisbane, police mounted a major operation to keep aborigines demonstrating for human rights away from the television cameras. Nothing was to divert us from the sight of a giant inflated kangaroo being paraded around to the strains of Rolf Harris singing 'Tie Me Kangaroo Down, Sport'.

The next Olympics are to be in Los Angeles in 1984. It will be interesting to see what measures the authorities use to keep black militants, gay rights activists or organised feminist groups out of the stadium and off the screen.

Once sport became a global television spectacle it provided a means for groups normally denied a public voice to make themselves heard. The outcome in 1972 was tragic.

During the Munich Olympics eight armed Palestinians occupied the Israeli quarters in the Olympic Village, killing one athlete and holding nine others hostage. They demanded the release of 200 Palestinian prisoners in Israel. After protracted negotiations five Palestinians and all the hostages died in a shoot-out with German security forces.

Even this traumatic episode did not disrupt the spectacle for more than a few hours. Amidst controversy, the International

Olympic Committee declared a day of mourning but timed it retroactively to start at 4 p.m. the previous day, apparently so the games could start again quickly. In the memorial service IOC president Avery Brundage outraged many by equating the massacre with the successful attempt to force the IOC to exclude Rhodesia that had preceded the games.

The Munich episode and the Moscow boycott had one thing in common: they both exploited the prominence of sport to make a political point. But in neither case did the political struggle specifically relate to sport itself. Unlike the struggle over apartheid, neither the Moscow boycott nor the Munich incident was an attempt to challenge the organisation of sport itself.

They were examples of the contact between politics and sport, a contact that is inevitable, as sport is part of society. The choice of sport to make a political point was, however, relatively arbitrary. It was determined by the prominence of sport in the public eye rather than by any intrinsic property of sport.

This book will concentrate, not on politics *and* sport, but upon the politics *of* sport. By this I mean the social organisation of sport, the institutions that govern it and the values invested in it. In particular, I want to look at the social base of these forms of organisation and values and at the extent to which they are contested rather than merely accepted.

Sport is difficult to explore precisely because it has so successfully preserved an apolitical appearance. There are no broadly accepted socialist principles, let alone strategies. There have been political struggles over leisure but they have had little in common.

Invading the pitch

One of the better-known incidents of suffragette history is the death of Emily Davison, a member of the Women's Social and Political Union. She died at the 1913 Derby when she threw hereself under the king's horse, Anmer, as it rounded Tattenham Corner. Her funeral was attended by 6,000 women.

This was only the most publicised of a series of incidents throughout 1913 as the suffragettes adopted a more militant stance. Many involved sport facilities. All over the country suffragettes tore up the turf of cricket and football grounds, bowling greens and golf clubs and burned buildings down.

The choice of sport as a target was not coincidental. Sport is a symbol of masculinity and male chauvinism. In attacking sport facilities the suffragettes were attacking a social institution rooted in male power.

Over fifty years later two black American sprinters chose the 1968 Mexico Olympics to make their statement to the world. Tommie Smith and John Carlos finished first and third in the 200 metres. They walked out to the medal ceremony each wearing one black glove. During the playing of the anthem they both looked down and held one fist aloft – the black power salute. Both the two Americans and silver medallist Peter Norman wore human rights badges.

The gesture was intended to highlight the contrast between the place of black people temporarily in the world spotlight and their place in society as a whole. As Tommie Smith pointed out, all his victory meant was that whereas before he was called a nigger, now he was a fast nigger.

It was particularly appropriate that this protest occurred at a sporting event. Like music, sport has often been represented as an arena in which black people can succeed – it is the mythical escape route from the ghetto. Even if the route were real it would merely divert attention from the oppression of black people in almost all other areas of social life. But black people also encounter prejudice and oppression within sport itself.

During the 1970s a number of campaigns developed in this country aimed specifically at the sporting world. The highly successful Anti-Nazi League was formed to combat the menace of fascism. Concern grew at the attempts of right-wing groups to recruit support at football grounds and a number of ANL offshoots developed to combat this (e.g. Spurs against the Nazis).

In 1977 another football-oriented campaign developed north of the border. The Scottish football team was scheduled to play Chile on a forthcoming South American tour. The venue was the notorious Santiago stadium, used as a concentration camp after the 1973 military coup which overthrew the Allende government. The campaign objected, without success, to both the visit and the venue.

The movement against hunting has a longer history and has continued to make inroads into this disgusting pastime. It has been able to persuade councils and some private landowners to bar hunts from their property. The adoption of sabotage techniques has helped to expose some of the arrogance, hypocrisy and underlying violence of the fox-hunting class.

Struggle over leisure is not a recent development. One of the largest campaigns over leisure provision developed in the 1930s. In 1932 500 people took part in a mass trespass on the Kinder Scout grouse moor in the Peak District, demanding public access. They were met by a gang of gamekeepers wielding sticks. Five were arrested. A subsequent ramblers' rally attracted 10,000.

The 1949 National Parks and Access to the Countryside Act was intended to open up the countryside but had little success. Existing public paths are constantly menaced by landowners and if anything the degree of public access to the countryside is declining. A 1974 survey of Oxfordshire found that only 111 of its 27,000 acres of woodland were open to the public.

The Sheffield Campaign for Access to Moorland celebrated the 50th anniversary of Kinder Scout with more mass trespasses in 1982. What Britain needs is an equivalent to the Swedish 'right to ramble' laws which give everyone the right to walk where no danger of damage or invasion of privacy exists.

Another campaign to emerge from Yorkshire is the Equal Rights in Clubs Campaign for Action (ERICCA), which is challenging the discrimination against women in club and institute union clubs. A majority of the 4,000 clubs operate a two-tier membership system. Most women cannot vote, stand for office, nominate others for office or use men-only rooms.

The campaign grew out of Sheila Capstick's struggle to be allowed to play snooker at her local club. She and her husband started a snooker for women campaign, with the slogan 'A woman's right to cues', and collected 2,000 signatures on a petition. Supporters of the campaign then set up ERICCA. But a recent private member's bill failed to amend the law to prevent discrimination in private clubs. Vera Selby is the women's world snooker champion and also the first woman snooker television commentator. Yet in her local league 11 of the 13 clubs are men only. So she must withdraw from away matches, allowing her opponents to claim the points by default.

These campaigns show that people are prepared to struggle over sport and leisure. But the support they have won and the success they have achieved have both been limited. One campaign, however, has succeeded both in gaining widespread support and in winning significant victories. In just over a decade the anti-apartheid movement secured a substantial isolation of South Africa in world sport. The fight to prevent these gains being eroded continues.

The apartheid system rests on legal apparatus which treats black and coloured people as second-class citizens. This is enforced by draconian police power. South Africa is a racialist police state. In the late 1950s the anti-apartheid movement began to identify sport as an area in which apartheid could be exposed and attacked. Bishop Trevor Huddleston did much to bring the issue into public debate in Britain.

In South Africa the South African Sports Association was formed in 1958 to promote black opportunity in sport. In 1962 the South African Non-Racial Olympic Committee (SANROC) was formed. The SASA secretary Denis Brutus was banned from teaching and journalism and from attending social and political gatherings. He could not be quoted in South Africa, was not allowed to leave Johannesburg, could not visit his family and had to report to the police every week.

He managed to leave South Africa in 1965 in an attempt to get to Baden-Baden to lobby the International Olympic Committee, but was captured by Portuguese security police and returned to South Africa. He was shot and seriously injured by Johannesburg police while trying to escape. By the mid-1960s repression had forced SASA to suspend its activities, and SANROC, along with Brutus himself, had been forced into exile in London. But SANROC did succeed in getting South Africa suspended from the 1964 Olympics.

Apartheid first became a major issue in Britain during the D'Oliviera affair. Basil D'Oliviera was a highly talented cricketer and a coloured South African who had been forced to leave and settle in England to pursue a cricket career. He was a contender for the MCC team to tour South Africa in 1968 but was not selected. There was widespread suspicion that he had been rejected in accordance with the wish of the South African government. A late injury to another player and pressure on the MCC then led to D'Oliviera's inclusion in the touring party. South Africa announced that he was unacceptable and after great turmoil the MCC called the tour off.

With the issue firmly in the public eye, the campaigns against apartheid were stepped up. A South African cricket tour was due to visit England in 1970 and Young Liberals, including Peter Hain, were active in forming the Stop The Seventy Tour campaign. Their first move was to organise a highly successful direct action campaign to disrupt the South African rugby tour of winter 1969–70. The matches were played to an accompaniment of chanted slogans, pitch invasions and struggles between demonstrators and police. The tour staggered through to a conclusion although halfway through the players voted to go home.

Although no matches were actually prevented, it was clear that the cricket tour was in grave doubt. (Cricket pitches are considerably more vulnerable than rugby grounds, as the 'George Davis Is Innocent OK' campaign later proved when it brought a test match to a premature conclusion by digging holes in the wicket.) Public and government pressure on the MCC mounted and even inside cricket there was growing opposition to South Africa. In May STST won their victory – the tour was cancelled.

This cancellation was only part of a major breakthrough in the struggle against apartheid. In 1970 South Africa was expelled from the Olympic movement and from the Davis Cup and was suspended from international athletics and gymnastics.

White South Africans, fanatical about sport, found this isolation hard to take. During the 1970s there were attempts to undermine international hostility to apartheid. The adoption of a 'multinational sport policy' allowed whites, Africans, blacks and Asians to compete, but only as four separate 'nations' within the country, and then only in competitions that also involved foreign teams. Mixed sport was still barred.

When this had little effect on international hostility, a co-option strategy, which attempted to include some black sport groups within the white sports structure, was developed. Some black sport bodies were absorbed by this. But the real stronghold of the anti-apartheid movement, the non-racial black sport organisations, saw through the policy and rejected co-option.

Apologists for apartheid argue that there is no law specifically prohibiting mixed sport. But there is a mass of legislation controlling the use of sport facilities and the movement of black people in sport. The pass laws can be effectively used to prevent black participation in sport except on terms dictated by the white authorities. Any pretence at 'normal' non-racial sport in such a society can only be a hollow sham.

Third world and socialist countries have orchestrated the international pressure on South Africa. The western nations have dragged their feet. The boycott threats that led to the expulsion of South Africa from the Olympic movement were led largely by African nations. It was not until the boycott of the 1976 Commonwealth Games that western nations were forced to declare their positions more clearly. Meeting in Britain in 1977, the Commonwealth Ministers drew up the Gleneagles agreement. This declared that it was the urgent duty of each government vigorously to combat the evil of apartheid by withholding any form of support for, and by taking every practical step to discourage, sporting contact with South Africa.

The South African response has been to offer huge sums to tempt sports competitors to tour. South African Breweries spent £1.2 million setting up the 1982 cricket tour that led to Geoffrey Boycott and Graham Gooch being banned from test cricket.

Another £1 million was spent on setting up a football tour later the same year. Despite reference to a range of star names, most of the players who actually toured were at the end of their careers. The tour became a farce. The party were met at Soweto airport by several hundred blacks chanting 'Rebels go home', three black teams pulled out of arranged matches and the tour was cut short.

The main problem currently facing the anti-apartheid movement in sport is the lack of enthusiasm shown by western nations, and particularly Britain, for implementing the spirit of the Gleneagles agreement. Neither the government nor the Sports Council has shown a lead.

The government says that it cannot interfere with the rights of independent sports organisations or individuals. Yet in 1980 in efforts to enforce a boycott of the Moscow Olympics it withheld foreign office co-operation, instructed the civil service and police to refuse to grant leave to Moscow-bound athletes and offered large sums of public money for alternative events.

While the Sports Council formally supports the Gleneagles agreement, it has done little to pressure those sports that maintain links with South Africa. The Rugby Football Union defied the government's expressed wish in approving a British Lions tour of South Africa in 1980. Yet the same year the Sports Council presented them with £500,000 towards a £3.4 million rebuilding project for Twickenham. Sports Council chairperson and ex-rugby player Dick Jeeps accepted an invitation to South Africa to be the guest speaker at the 1980 Sports Greats Awards. By contrast, black Sports Council member Paul Stephenson, who is rather more critical of apartheid, was refused admission to South Africa.

In the absence of a clear lead from governments the United Nations Register of Sports Contacts with South Africa has become an important means of maintaining pressure. The register lists organisations and individuals who maintain sporting links with South Africa.

The anti-apartheid movement has been of great importance. The sporting isolation of South Africa has been a highly successful political campaign. It has kept apartheid a prominent issue worldwide and has prevented South Africa from masking its oppression with a veneer of normality. It has also been powerful enough to cause changes in South African sporting policy. Even though these changes are little more than cosmetic, they help to maintain the pressure upon the whole apartheid system. South Africa is now caught in a dilemma. It has tried to create the impression of a relaxation of apartheid by producing pseudo multi-racial sport organisation at national level, while continuing the brutal repression unabated in social life.

The various struggles outlined here challenge the view that sport is a world of its own. They treat the social organisation of sport as part of that of society as a whole. But they do not amount to a coherent strategy. They are not informed by an overall socialist attitude to sport.

Standing on the sidelines

Most socialists don't take sport very seriously. It is not seen as a site of struggle, nor even as a very significant part of social life. In part this is a product of the labour movement's traditional focus on economic and political struggle.

The core of much socialist analysis is the class struggle. For many this struggle takes place at the workplace, in confrontation between worker and boss. Other forms of politics are peripheral. Victory is to be sought in workplace organisation and victory is inevitable because sooner or later workers will realise where their true class interest lies.

The failure of socialism to become genuinely popular in the 1950s and 1960s was attributed to rising affluence. Wait until the next crisis, the pundits said, and a more radical mood will develop. For a time in the early 1970s this scenario seemed to be coming true. There were massive mobilisations to fight industrial relations legislation, culminating in the defeat of the Heath government by the 1974 miners' strike.

But recent developments are more disturbing. The adoption of hard-line monetarist economic policy, extensive cuts in public spending and an engineered rise in unemployment to nearly four million have failed to produce an upsurge in socialist consciousness.

Despite the very real decline in the living standards and the very bleak prospects facing working people, the Thatcher government appears to be popular, even with people who suffer most from current government policies.

The labour movement has to confront the failure of socialism to become a popular force. The question of consciousness – what people think about the world and why – is central. Working-class people do not automatically turn to socialism any more than women automatically turn to feminism.

Socialists have always been aware of this problem. The last 15 years have seen a growth of interest in problems of ideology – of how people in subordinate classes come to consent to, and acquiesce in, class domination. There has been a mounting interest in the media and other cultural institutions and in the part they play in shaping people's understanding of the world. This interest has led to a developed critique of the media and of the dominant culture. Analyses of the media have attempted to investigate the way that consensus is maintained, the way that a particular view of social reality is reproduced, and the way trade unionists, women, blacks and other groups are presented in a stereotypical manner.

New forms of cultural struggle have confronted this pattern of domination. The opening up of a range of alternatives – the radical press, independent cinema and fringe theatre – has attempted to challenge the power of dominant voices. The existing practices of media production have come under greater pressure from anti-racist and anti-sexist campaigns. Struggle to make greater space for alternative views has taken place around, for example, the formation of Channel Four.

The growth of interest in culture has enlivened socialist debate in a variety of fields – the press, cinema, television and publishing. But sport remains largely neglected.

This neglect is part of a broader pattern. The socialist tradition generally gives physical matters a low status. The body has been seen as a personal, individualised concern, somehow apart from society. Only in debates about the health services does the physical side of life figure and then only in a marginal fashion.

The rise of feminism has challenged this blind spot. The insistence that the personal is political, that social practices structure people's physical lives and that sexuality and relations between men and women are political, has begun to transform the place of the physical in socialism. Childcare, nursery provision, women's right to abortion on demand and the nature of health care are all, quite rightly, being pushed to greater prominence on the labour movement's agenda.

But even within feminism there has been surprisingly little discussion of sport. Sport has traditionally been such a bastion of maleness that it offers a perfect site for a critical exposure of the culture of masculinity. But the redefinition of femininity being produced by the strength of the women's movement has also begun to transform sport. Women are increasingly prepared to challenge male definitions of their capabilities. The growth in women's marathon running is only the most publicised example.

There are also deeper reasons for the neglect of sport as an aspect of social life. Just as there is a division between mental and manual labour, so there is a division between mental and physical activity. English cultural life is marked by a very distinct division between two types of person – the sporting philistine and the non-sporting aesthete. These are the two archetypal products of the English public school and university education. One is the hearty muscular sportster, manly, friendly and insensitive, who knows nothing of art, music or literature. The other is the sensitive aesthete who finds energetic physical activity vulgar.

So sporting clture is, compared to that of many other countries, intellectually empty, and our artistic life has no sense of physical dynamism. Sport is marked down as a natural, taken-for-granted activity. You don't need to talk or write about it. You just do it.

This division between the mental and physical has its impact on the left. Am I alone, when sitting in damp meeting halls in clouds of cigarette smoke gazing around at the sea of drawn faces, slumped shoulders and pot bellies, in wondering how many of us are going to be alive when the revolution comes? How many will be fit enough to storm the barricades?

It is a great irony that we who would fight against capitalist exploitation are so often unable to combat its destruction of our own bodies with products like tobacco. We need to recognise that capitalism has deformed more than just our working relations. The right to a fit, healthy existence should be an integral part of the struggle for socialism. We cannot afford to treat the physical as peripheral.

Because physicality is marginalised in this way, socialists tend to comment on sport only when it is overtly political. So socialist writing on sport has a rather one-dimensional character.

It has consistently sought to assert that you cannot keep politics out of sport, that sport is not a world of its own but a part of social life. It has been less successful in exploring the complex and contradictory nature of the politics of sport.

I think there are five reasons why socialists should take sport more seriously. First, there is a need to avoid the traps of the past. There are great dangers in focusing too narrowly on industrial struggle. Relations between capitalists and workers in the factory may indeed be crucial, but not to the exclusion of all else. Many of the areas in which socialist organisation has most successfully caught the popular imagination recently have been aspects of cultural struggle – the anti-fascist movement, the fight against sexist representations of women, rock against racism, and so on. We need to take all aspects of social life seriously, especially popular cultural forms like sport.

Second, the way people see the world presents major problems for socialism. To build a genuinely popular movement we need to develop and spread a socialist way of looking at the world, and dislodge the dominance of the bourgeois world-view.

Sport as it exists in this country contributes to the way people see the world. We need to work out how to engage with this problem. Is it possible to work for a non-racist, non-sexist, non-nationalistic and more co-operative form of sport? Or should the whole institution of sport merely be exposed and attacked?

Third, physical well-being, health and fitness are important to human development. Socialism should be a way of making a healthier life possible for all. It should make clear that capitalism inhibits the possibility of universal fitness. Some forms of sport could be an important element in the path to greater health and fitness.

Fourth, play and pleasure are also important in human development. The old Salvation Army adage was 'Why should the devil have all the best tunes?' We need to start asking, 'Why should the bosses have all the best games?' There are great dangers in appearing too puritan about fun. Play in some form will be an important element of a more fulfilling society. We need to see what possibilities lie in more playful forms of sport.

Finally, mechanisation, new technology and electronics have already begun to transform the nature of work. Physical labour is on the decline. At present these changes are used primarily to create more profit, with the by-product of large-scale permanent unemployment. The much-touted leisure society is already here for four million on the dole. The only problem is that they've given us the leisure and kept the money.

But even if unemployment is tackled, shorter working hours will mean more leisure time. Leisure will become an increasingly politicised issue. Battles will be fought over who has leisure time, how it is spent and how it is provided for. Socialists should intervene in these debates and be active in struggles.

The questions raised here are difficult and there is no merit in quick, glib answers. This book is intended to open a debate – to place sport and physical leisure on the socialist agenda – and not to provide instant solutions.

The second chapter surveys some socialist critiques of sport. The institutions of sport have been attacked for being a form of distraction, a tool of the state, a part of capitalist business and a part of bourgeois ideology. These critiques are valuable but only as a starting point.

Chapter Three outlines the historical development of the institutions of English sport, showing how the major sporting institutions came to be dominated by a stratum of the male bourgeoisie. Chapter Four examines the development of sport as large-scale entertainment reproduced as spectacle for television, the degree of resistance to this process and the existence of possible alternatives.

The last two chapters examine state policy and socialist alternatives. Chapter Five suggests that England has always lacked a
coherent direction in sport policy and that the private sector is
increasingly likely to fill the vacuum. Chapter Six outlines various
options to be considered in any attempt to develop a socialist
strategy for sport.

2.

Arguments about Sport

Not many socialists have taken an interest in discussion of sport. But the few who have written on the subject have produced lively and trenchant criticism. Sport has been attacked as a distraction, a way of providing a safety valve and keeping the masses quiet, as an arm of the state and a way of building nationalism, as a part of capitalist business and as a form of bourgeois ideology.

This chapter will outline what socialists have said about sport and its forms of organisation. These criticisms are important if we are not simply to take sport for granted as a natural activity. They seek to challenge much of the existing common sense concerning sport, which is a combination of idealism and an apolitical liberalism. To appreciate these criticisms we must first look briefly at these conventional attitudes towards sport.

The idealist view of sport has some of its roots in Greek attitudes. It relates sport to physical perfection and sees athletic endeavour as the body striving for perfection. One variant of this view is the concept of physical and mental harmony. A rather more influential one is the concept of the healthy mind in the healthy body. Consistent improvement in sport performance is seen as an indicator of human progress. The emphasis on records and measurement is even enshrined in the Olympic motto – 'Faster, Higher, Stronger'.

A rather different variant stresses the importance of play, which is seen as non-purposive activity important to human development. The ability to have fun is viewed as a fundamental human trait. There are two rather different ways of applying this notion to sport. Some hold that sport is essentially irrational and so a form of play. Others argue that sport represents the more organised, rational, and consequently negative form of play. Most popular sports are played at very informal levels – street football, beach cricket, tennis against a wall, childrens' races – and may here be closer to play than in their more organised forms. The opponents of professional sport often argue that at the highest level all the fun has gone because here people take sport too seriously.

The classic liberal/apolitical view is that sport is a world of its own, apart from the rest of social life. It is full of fun, excitement, drama and involvement. But it has nothing to do with the real world and should be shielded from it. In other words, keep politics out of sport. This view wrongly assumes that the existing organisation of sport is non-political and opposes any external interference (except government funding, ideally with no strings attached). For 'Keep politics out of sport' read 'Keep the politics of sport the way they are'.

A cultural approach is directly opposed to this apolitical one in that, far from attempting to separate sport from social life, it seeks to emphasise the relation between the two. The significance of particular sports is then located in the way that the culture surrounding a particular sport expresses the social values of those involved. So football is seen as deeply embedded in the social and cultural experience of urban working-class man. The solidarity within the crowd, the local loyalties, the conventions of tough physicality, and the particular forms of humour, all stem from the basic connection between football and its social roots.

This last position bring us much closer to a socialist analysis of sport. Clearly, in order to understand sports fully, it is crucial to situate them within their social and historical contexts. Socialist analysis raises a whole set of questions about the nature of this context. How does sport relate to the development of industrial capitalism? What place does sport have within the state apparatus? To what extent is sport part of the dominant ideology – the system of ideas that work to perpetuate class domination? Does socialism need sport?

The rest of this chapter will examine four types of socialist critique, in which sport is attacked as a distraction, as an arm of the state, as a part of capitalism and as a form of ideology.

Bread and circuses

There is a long tradition of viewing sport and leisure as distractions, keeping the oppressed masses from more disruptive activity. Leisure time is seen as that time spent outside working hours when people are temporarily free of labour discipline and so relatively unoppressed. The idea that some form of excitement might distract people from their mean conditions is not new. The Roman emperors believed they could keep the masses quiet with bread and circuses.

Some recent socialist thought has seen sport as a form of circus, a gaudy spectacle. Just as religion was once the opium of the people, now it is sport that narcotises the working classes. Traditionally, religion provided elaborate venues, separate from the rest of social life, in the form of churches. Inside, idols and mythical figures were worshipped and a series of rituals, spread through the calendar, were performed. Today the stadiums of sport, equally separate from social life, provide the venues for worshipping stars. Sport has its own rituals throughout the calendar – the Cup Final, the Boat Race, the Grand National and so on.

The growth of television on a global scale has accelerated this tendency, creating the society of the spectacle. The world is increasingly dominated by elaborate spectacles which serve to mask the ruthless exploitation of the existing economic order. Life is seen through television. A world of passive spectators rooted to the screen is pacified by ever more elaborate entertainment, spectacular yet devoid of any real substance. All events become reduced to the same level – coronations, moon shots, assassinations, elections, World Cups, papal visits, Olympic Games, wars – all become part of the great global television show.

If social reality cannot be absorbed within the spectacle then it must be excluded. The coverage of the World Cup in Argentina managed to avoid comment on the brutal military dictatorship. Television commentators assured us that they had been made very welcome. In the light of the subsequent Falklands war, television's silence on the subject of the fascist junta and the 'disappearance' of thousands of Argentine citizens is deeply ironic.

Presenting sport as a world of its own enables the media neatly to bracket out other events. The killing of 1,000 demonstrators by Mexican authorities just before the 1968 Olympics was quietly forgotten once the games started. Only in 1972, when the Palestinian seizing of Israeli hostages and subsequent deaths disrupted the flow of the games themselves, was the spectacle briefly dislodged.

The importance of sport is grotesquely inflated by its place in the global spectacle. During the 1982 World Cup there were strong hints in the media that an England win would provide a third great event, to go along with the birth of the royal baby and the Falklands victory. This bizarre suggestion was most apparent in those papers which insist most strongly that politics must be kept out of sport.

It is not only at the level of television spectacle that sport can be seen as a distraction. Many people in the sports world, battling for years for adequate financing for inner-city projects, have discovered that, since Brixton and Toxteth, the easiest way to get funding has been to mutter grimly about riots.

Involvement in sport is seen as a diversion, keeping the working class, and particularly the black working class, from engaging in class struggle. Were they not spending their time on the terraces, watching the box or in sports halls, so the argument goes, they might be out seizing state power.

Just as this view alarms the establishment, it attracts the left. It is easy to see why. The spectacle of 20,000 people behind the goal at a football match chanting 'Come on, you reds' is both intriguing and frustrating. All that energy wasted on 22 men and a bag of wind. What might 20,000 Liverpool workers achieve if they travelled up and down the country for socialism instead of football? How might South American dictators tremble if they heard 10,000 Scots heading their way, not for a football match, but to pursue enquiries about missing trade unionists? The fantasy is beguiling.

But it is a fantasy. The failure to win people to socialist activity cannot simply be blamed on the other activities that fill their time. Football crowds have slumped drastically with massive unemployment. Yet no whirlwind of socialist struggle has arisen in football towns.

When all is blamed on 'distractions', people are seen simply as mindless dupes and their use of leisure as manipulation by the ruling class. In reality, people make choices in their lives. Of course the fact that we make choices does not mean that we get what we want. We choose from a limited set of options determined largely by forces beyond our control. The pattern of work determines the amount of time and money available to us. The range of options is limited by the operation of the leisure industry and the nature of state provision. But if socialism currently fails to galvanise the working class of Liverpool, it is not because 90 minutes of football are played every week.

Sport and the state

Attempts at social control are not the only close links between sport and the state. Sport is closely associated with the military in many countries. It has been used to boost national fitness in preparation for war. It has close associations with the monarchy and various sports are an important part of the royal family's public image. International sport has always been manipulated according to the needs of diplomacy. The English empire and its attitudes to other races affected the development of international sport. Sport is also important in the self-image of most nations.

Sport has traditionally been seen as a way of boosting patriotism. In 1773 Rousseau said that games should be used to create a deep love for the nation. After the Napoleonic wars, Friedrich Jahn, a founding figure of gymnastics, said that a national sporting movement could regenerate the German people. A century later Nazi generals were to see sport as a form of military service. Much of the Soviet Union's sporting success, notably the Moscow Dynamo football team, grew out of the KGB's sport organisation. In pre-revolutionary China games were used to build people's health to fight imperialism.

In Britain sport has been important to the public schools in their role of providing an officer class. The famous poem 'Vita Lampada' ('There's a breathless hush in the close tonight . . .') directly links the skills needed to inspire a cricket team with those used to rally an imperialist army. Team sport was held to foster and develop leadership qualities needed by the empire. This system provided officers, but the establishment worried periodically about the state of the potential 'other ranks'.

The concept of national fitness has different implications in different contexts. The mass fitness programme of Nazi Germany and the sport-for-all policies of the German Democratic Republic are only superficially similar. In Britain, war usually triggers off a sudden interest in the physical fitness of the proletariat. These worries surfaced after the Crimean war, during the Boer war and before the first and second world wars. But attempts to remedy the problem were seldom successful.

There were a number of reasons. First, the fear that national fitness was inadequate never really gripped the ruling class as a whole. Second, especially before universal secondary education, the state lacked adequate machinery to promote programmes for national fitness. Third, there were differences within physical education over the value of physical training as opposed to games as such. There was also some mutual hostility between military-trained drill teachers and college-trained physical education teachers. Fourth, there has always been a substantial degree of resistance to organised physical activity amongst the people. The system of sport in Britain has a strong *ad hoc* improvised character to it. The attempt to boost national fitness in the late 1930s was widely considered a failure. When the second world war started, fears over fitness were seen to be largely unfounded.

After the second world war the expansion of the welfare state provided the machinery for boosting national fitness. But the long-term future of the military was now seen in a technological light. National fitness became associated more with the need for a healthy productive workforce, to be reared on free milk, orange juice and organised games.

Sport and the state are also linked through the involvement of the monarchy. The British royal family follows the aristocratic leisure tradition. Its members prefer hunting, racing and equestrian sports. But they have taken care to associate themselves with more popular events by ritual appearances on occasions like the Cup Final.

They leave their mark in peculiar ways. The marathon is a foot race lasting 26 miles and 385 yards. This odd distance is generally believed to commemorate the carrying of a message in the Battle of Marathon. In fact the marathon used to be run over 26 miles. The extra 385 yards were added so that the 1908 Olympic marathon, which started at Windsor Castle, could finish opposite the royal box at White City Stadium.

Royalty have shaped international sport much more than is generally realised. During the 1960s the self-electing International

Olympic Committee, supreme authority over the Olympic Games, had among its members Prince Alexandre of Belgium, Prince Georg of Hanover, Prince Cholum of Iran, Prince Tsunfyoski Takeda of Japan, Prince Franz Josef II of Lichtenstein, Grand Duke Jean of Luxembourg and King Constantine of Greece.

International sport is often the tool of diplomacy. The Football Association has taken instructions from the Foreign Office as to which countries to visit and which to avoid. In 1938 the England team visited Germany and, despite protests from the players, were instructed by the FA to give the Nazi salute in the pre-match line-up. Sadly, as England were eliminated from the 1982 World Cup, we will never know if the Thatcher government would have taken the politically unpopular move of withdrawing rather than playing Argentina so soon after the Falklands war.

The state looms large where national image is concerned. International sport has always been a battle for national self-pride, a war without weapons. Sporting success has been regarded as a matter for national self-congratulation, failure as a matter for state concern.

Newly independent nations have devoted great energy and resources to sport as a way of establishing themselves on the international stage. The communist countries of eastern Europe consciously adopted a policy of proving communist superiority by outstripping the western nations in Olympic performance, a goal which they have achieved remarkably successfully.

Western media lay great emphasis on competition at the national level. The fate of the England football team is taken as a symbol of national well-being. Harold Wilson, having attempted to identify himself with the England World Cup victory of 1966, hoped to retain office in a quiet election in 1970 timed to coincide with the World Cup. Unfortunately England and Harold were both eliminated.

This prominence of sport in the English national identity was heightened by arrogance. For years the English assumed that their football team was the best in the world. They held aloof from the World Cup when it was launched in 1930, preferring to challenge the victors at their leisure. This assumption was not to be rudely shattered until the 1950s; first, when during England's first World Cup in 1950 they were beaten by the USA, a nation with no tradition of playing football, and, second, when Hungary came to

Wembley in 1953 and won 6–3. The myth of national superiority was also undermined by increasing American and Russian dominance in the Olympics.

The quest for international success became a concern of the state and a rallying call of those within sport pressing for greater funding. But the involvement of the British state in sport has been somewhat half-hearted. The overwhelming proportion of funding is at a municipal level. There has rarely been a coherent national policy or an adequate level of funding.

No business like sport business

A rather different form of critique emphasises the penetration of sport by business. It argues that sport is owned and controlled by the capitalist class and run like a business. Its internal organisation is hierarchical. It has a highly developed division of labour. Its techniques are designed to extract maximum productivity from its performers. It is increasingly dominated by the need to be profitable or at least to avoid losses. Its potential for promotional activity and the growth of sponsorship are increasingly transforming it into a branch of the advertising industry.

Organised sport in Britain exists within a capitalist society. So it is constrained by the economic and social relations particular to capitalism.

But it is a simplification to say that sport is run like a business. Take the case of professional football. Probably the sport with most potential for profit, it currently faces severe economic problems. While clubs operate as limited companies, they have not been run predominantly for profit. Indeed Football League restrictions limit the distribution of surplus in the form of dividends.

Clubs have been controlled mainly by local businessmen, not for gain so much as for power and influence in the community and as a hobby. Some would suggest that many of football's problems stem precisely from the fact that it is *not* run as a business.

The striking thing about the organisation of many British sports is that they have remained cushioned from economic pressures for so long by a combination of insularity, conservatism, exploitation of voluntary labour, amateurism and hostility to commercialism. It is only in the last 20 years that this rather cosy, enclosed world has been penetrated much by harsh economic realities. Pressures towards commerce and profit have largely come from outside the structure of British sport – from televisions, sponsors, agents and advertising.

The organisation of British sport has been hierarchical. A top layer of elderly, male administrators holds power over most sports. A middle stratum of managers, coaches and trainers also exercises substantial control over players. In football the manager, always called 'the boss', has become, via the media, the pivotal figure of the game. The boss wields complete power over players, yet can be, and frequently is, sacked at a moment's notice by the board of directors.

There is a widening gap between the few star players who can receive vast amounts in pay and fringe earnings, and the rest, who are often fairly badly paid. If they fail to make the grade they can find themselves unemployed and unemployable in their late 20s.

Below the players and performers come the ranks of unseen workers who help to make sports possible. The recent strikes of stable lads revealed to the public the appalling rates of pay and conditions typical of this level of sport labour.

At the top, training methods are geared to obtaining maximum productivity from the human body. Great stress is laid on work rate, commitment and dedication. Top athletes have to cross the pain threshold constantly. This type of training has been compared to the time and motion methods used to obtain maximum productivity in industry.

In many ways sport *is* a form of business. The crisis facing many traditional amateur organisations has made financial survival a key concern. Many have responded by stepping up sales in club shops, squeezing more from catering concessions, aiming at a family audience (that is, middle-class consumers) and opening potentially lucrative leisure centres. The growth of television, and consequent massive expansion of sponsorship, has led many to see today's sport as a branch of the advertising industry.

But, if sports are businesses, they are businesses of a very particular kind. In most British sports the need to make a profit, or at least avoid a loss, is not the main motive. Most of the people involved see it as a regrettable necessity.

The tradition of amateur paternalism is still strong in British sport. Many people are more interested in control and power than in money. There is often a tension between the money-making potential at the top and the needs of the grassroots. Many governing bodies are fighting a battle, often a losing one, to redistribute some of the wealth available at sport's highest levels.

A sporting idea

Sport offers a way of seeing the world. It is part of the system of ideas that supports, sustains and reproduces capitalism. It offers a way of seeing the world that makes our very specific form of social organisation seem natural, correct and inevitable.

Sport does this in four main ways. It presents a series of ideas about the relation of individuals to spectacle, of active and passive behaviour, of the relation of elite performers to mass audiences. It also presents a way of seeing our nation and the nations of others. The values of the sport world stress individual endeavour and achievement. And sport offers a model of the relation between men and women.

Sport provides spectacles. In the twentieth century sport has come to mean spectator sport to most people. The handful of players are greatly outnumbered by the millions who watch. We have become a world of televiewers.

We are passive consumers, entertained by a small elite of stars. Our attention is increasingly focused on the highest level. Sports meetings find it more and more important to have stars, made familiar by television, to attract crowds. A major distinction grows up between *us*, the mass of passive consumers, and *them*, the active elite.

As in sport, so in politics. *They* are the actors, the people who appear on the screen to make news, control events and so make history. *We* are the people who gaze at them in awe and wonder.

But sport also offers a way out of passive individualism. It offers us a greater collectivity to identify with, a way of feeling less of a lone individual. It offers us the team, the county and above all the nation. National sport is a powerful component of national symbolism.

Many people who laugh at the monarchy identify with their national football or cricket team. Terms like English or British derive much of their significance from national sporting traditions. Sport provides us with a sense of belonging to a nation, however irrational that may be.

Sports also reinforces stock stereotypes of other nations. Italians are temperamental. The French are over-excited and a bit incompetent. Russians are dour and unsmiling, South Americans are unpredictable and violent. West Indians are flamboyant and undisciplined. East Germans are over-disciplined and unsmiling. Africans are enthusiastic but lack concentration.

Our images of Britishness are reinforced by sporting comparisons with other nations. The force of all this is heightened by the way that Britain for years sustained its notions of natural superiority based on the empire. Everyone else is held to smile too much or not enough when compared to us.

Within this comforting feeling of national unity, sport offers a model of the place of individuals. It provides a series of success stories – people who have achieved all the glories and rewards. We ignore failure and focus on winners. And these winners did not get where they are through unfair advantage, through accidents of birth. They got there through unremitting hard work, relentless application and commitment.

This is the message of the constant stress on work-rate and commitment. Anyone can make it but you have to work hard. You don't just work hard, you work harder than anyone else. Then you succeed in competition. You are prepared to go through the pain threshold more often, to give your all. At the same time you follow the commands of your boss, who knows best.

This notion of sport success provides a role model for the ideal worker, though an 'efficient' worker wouldn't reap the same rewards. It also offers a model for the struggling small business owner.

This view is supplemented with the rather contradictory notion of 'natural talent'. Hard work put sport stars where they are, but they also happen to be naturally gifted. It is all down to fate. Some have talent. Some do not. The rest of us are lucky to be able to watch the action replay on television.

Natural talent is never enough of course. George Best and John Conteh are salutary reminders of what happens to those who don't work hard to preserve their talent.

Sport also offers us a way of living by presenting particular notions of maleness and femaleness. In Britain sport culture is deeply embedded in traditional notions of masculinity. The stress on toughness, commitment, competitiveness, aggression and courage in sport all fit neatly into the traditional notion of 'being a man'.

Sporting activity is an important part of a boy's schooling. If you take part you are accepted as one of the chaps, a real man. If you reject sport, doubts are raised about your masculinity. Sport both defines and completes the image of maleness.

Girls pass through school rather differently. Sport is often as popular with girls as with boys until early in secondary school. From then on notions of femininity intervene. The impact of images of femininity leads many girls to reject sport as inappropriate. Girls who continue with it are often seen as a bit deviant, just like boys who reject sport.

So sport is part of the proces of defining differences between men and women. Men are supposed to play it, women are not. So men who reject sport and women who pursue it find that their sexuality is questioned.

This fits in with broader definitions of male and female. Boys are active, girls passive. Men do, women watch. The media find it difficult to treat women simply as sports people. They constantly refer back to their prettiness or lack of prettiness, to their husbands and children. Active physical activity is for men. Women who succeed in sport are treated as unusual. Sport both generates and reinforces a very traditional image of the difference between men and women. This helps to sustain male power.

The ideologies expressed through sport and the practice of sport reinforce each other in a vicious circle. Sport powerfully suggests itself as a male activity, so few girls persist with it. Few women then reach the public eye. The facts then confirm the image that sport is for men.

This pattern has been undermined in the last decade. Women have always been active in sport, although their involvement has typically been underplayed by the male focus of media coverage. But the success of the women's movement in dislodging traditional attitudes to femininity has changed attitudes to women's involvement in sport.

Women's sporting achievements are growing apace. But these successes require struggle against male-defined and -controlled structures, in sport and in society as a whole.

This struggle helps to undermine the existing ideology. Ideas about society are not simply transmitted from the dominant class to subordinate ones. There is always struggle over the power to define social reality. Certain ideas are dominant in sport, but they are not the only ones around. Women in sport are increasingly powerfully challenging the ways that men have portrayed them.

Stop the game or change the rules?

One conclusion drawn from these four lines of attack is that sport is not worth reforming. It has no place in a socialist society and should simply be exposed as a male-dominated, capitalist institution. I reject this argument. Before saying why, however, I will outline the bases of an anti-sport position.

There are really two rather different positions. Both emphasise the negative character of competition. The first sees competition as inherently capitalist. Competition in sport is treated as an analogy of competition in capitalism. Just as socialism will eliminate the need for competition between capitalist businesses, so it will eliminate any need for competition in sport. So sport will wither and die.

The second position sees competition as an inherent feature of masculinity and its prominence in our society as an effect of male dominance. If patriarchy is overthrown, competition will no longer be a socially important activity.

There clearly are close links between the values of sport and the place of the individual in capitalism. The individual is in competition with other individuals to achieve. Success is rated highly and people who achieve become celebrated. World records are a form of fetish-creation, which extracts a product from the labour of athletic endeavour – the record and the statistic. These figures then take on an independent existence as marks against which others must compete.

This process has been particularly noticeable in world athletics recently. The boom in middle-distance running inspired by Coe and Ovett has involved highly constructed paced record attempts and a decline in tactical racing.

The emphasis in sport on the need for hard work, individual sacrifice and the winning of rewards certainly matches the capitalist ideal of achievement. After all, sport does depend upon beating someone, proving yourself superior. For every winner, there is at least one loser.

Similarly the social construction of men in our society has produced a competitiveness particular to masculinity. The drive to success, to earn more, dress more expensively, to drive a faster car and so be seen with the most beautiful women is at the root of the images of maleness which surround us.

Sport is very central to being a 'real' man. To be good at sport is to be strong, powerful, virile and macho. To be bad at sport is to be inadequate as a man. In sport you prove yourself more of a man than your opponents.

If society was not so dominated by men and by the values of masculinity then competitive sport could not assume the huge cultural importance that it has at present. Overthrowing patriarchal domination would gradually transform social and cultural forms in such a way that competitive sport would have no place.

These are strong arguments. To be anti-sport is not simply to be negative. It is possible to argue for a non-competitive physical culture and for the development of non-competitive games. There are several books of children's games that do not involve competition and stress co-operation.

But the main problem with the anti-sport arguments is that they assume there is one essential property called 'competitiveness' to which all sports can be reduced. This property is then condemned as being irredeemably capitalist and/or patriarchal.

This book argues that competition takes many different forms. Boxing involves a different form than long jumping. Tennis in the park is different from tennis at the Wimbledon final. There is no single thing called competition that can be condemned or accepted.

The analogy with competition in capitalism is ultimately unhelpful. People are trying to beat each other in sport, but they are not trying to take each other over, or eliminate competition. There is no tendency to monopoly. Capitalist businesses aim to dominate their market totally. Total and permanent domination in sport renders a competition meaningless. The Football League clubs compete with each other but also depend on each other, for the structure of competition to continue. Competitive sport in a capitalist society does of course share the character of that society. But competition is not simply a product of capitalism.

Similarly the fact that competitiveness is a distinctive masculine trait in our society does not mean that it is an inevitable male characteristic. Competitive masculinity is not a biological fact. It is a social construction. It can change and be changed. Indeed many would argue that it is in escaping from traditional notions of feminine passivity and becoming more self-assertive that the women's movement has been able to confront sexism and chauvinism. Just as assertiveness can be positive or negative in different contexts, competition can take positive or negative forms.

Although ultimately wrong, the anti-sport arguments do invite us to look more closely at the idea of competition. Desires to lift a heavier weight, swim the butterfly stroke faster, knock other people out, or throw 16 lb lumps of metal about are rather peculiar. They are social products, rather than natural ways of behaving.

Certain forms of society emphasise competition. Others do not. If society is changed then the importance accorded to competition might well change too.

There was extensive debate about this in the Soviet Union during the decade following the revolution. Many health workers argued for the importance of a non-competitive physical culture based upon health and fitness. The first Trade Union Games in 1925 barred the highly popular sports of weightlifting, boxing, football and gymnastics. The Proletarian Cultural and Educational Organisation fought for the rejection of competitive sport, which they saw as the product of a degenerate bourgeois culture.

These tendencies were ultimately unsuccessful. Instead the Soviet Union turned to sport as a way of developing national fitness and identity, a policy that began to bring great international successes in the post-war era. The significance of this clearly depends upon broader political judgements about the Soviet system beyond the scope of this book. But it is worth noting that cultural change does not mirror political change in an automatic fashion.

Just as competition takes a variety of forms, so does sport. There is no single thing called sport, but rather a variety of competitive physical activities which we regard as sports. The word sport is a convenient label with which to generalise. To understand the development of sports in our society it is necessary to be more specific about the varied forms that sport takes.

There are three rather different ways in which the word is used. First, to refer to games themselves – the sets of rules and principles that govern their playing. Second, the term also designates the social institutions of sport – the clubs, stadiums and governing organisations within which sports take place. The third meaning refers to the cultural and social settings and to the attitudes that constitute various sports. Football is not simply a game with rules, clubs and stadiums. It also has a complex culture. Street football, Sunday morning games, big crowds, buying programmes, eating peanuts, chanting, fighting between rival supporters, discussing the game and watching it on television are all part of football.

To understand sport as a part of society we need to examine these three aspects and the relation between them more closely. The next two chapters give a brief account of the development of sporting institutions in England and the cultures that surround them.

3.

Ruling English Games

The last quarter of the twentieth century was the crucial period in English sport. Many of the major sport institutions were formed then and the class control that would shape English sport in the twentieth century was consolidated. It is in this sense that the period 1875–1900 saw the formation of English sport as we know it today. This chapter outlines the social processes leading up to that formation. The following one traces the growth of sport in the twentieth century.

The history of sport and leisure in England is in part the story of attempts by dominant classes to control the leisure time of subordinate classes and the story of attempts by men to control the leisure time of women. It is also the story of resistance to this control, marked by the persistent survival of popular activities.

Land ownership has always been a source of power. From the time of the Norman Conquest, the nobility enjoyed hunting for sport over huge tracts of land. Brutal penalties were imposed on peasants who killed for food rather than fun. The whole mechanism of hunting rights persists today with a thriving trade in shooting and fishing facilities in the Scottish highlands.

Laws affecting leisure have frequently treated different classes differently. The hunting laws extended the property rights of the nobility to wildlife. The cruel sports of the common people – bull-baiting and cock-fighting – were outlawed in the nineteenth century, while those of the aristocracy – hunting and shooting – remain legal today. Gambling laws have generally clamped down on betting amongst common people while leaving the gentry free to wager. Periodic attempts were made to enforce regular archery practice at the expense of bowls or football.

The power of men to define the place of women has affected women of all classes. Responsibility for domestic labour tends to mean that women simply do not have leisure time in the way that men do. Domestic labour and child-rearing tend to be never-ending forms of labour. Upper-class women, freed of domestic labour by servants, had access to some forms of leisure but the rise of Victorian attitudes to femininity mitigated against physical activity. The influence of puritan and evangelical moral codes made it hard for women even to adopt suitable clothing for sport. Working-class women in the nineteenth century frequently had both paid labour outside the home and unpaid labour within it.

But all these pressures were resisted. Popular festivals were an important part of social life for three hundred years, despite the power of the Puritan movement. Sports like bowls survived long periods of illegality. Women have persistently fought for the right to control their own lives.

This chapter examines the rich tradition of popular festivals and feast days and the eventual decline of rural recreations and urban pastimes. It discusses the public school cult of athleticism and the re-shaping of sport in the nineteenth century. It offers an account of the formation of English sport and the crucial control exerted by men of the Victorian middle classes.

Pre-industrial festivities

England had a rich tradition of festivals and feast days, such as May Day, stretching back many centuries. Food, drink, dancing and sport were all part of the regular celebrations. Women and children often played as active a role as men. Many of the sports were violent; cock-fighting, shin-kicking, bull-baiting and dog-tossing all seem to have been popular.

But recorded histories often disapproved of popular pastimes and so exaggerated the less savoury elements. There were many less violent activities. Running, stoolball, football, throwing at hoops, grinning contests and climbing the greasy pole have all been recorded as popular.

Women often took part in stoolball, shuttlecock and smock races, in which the runner was awarded with a smock. The participation of women was often exploited for sexual display, as it provided a ready-made excuse for brief clothing.

One of the best-known celebrations was the Cotswold games. The games dated back to Saxon times but were revived with much success by Robert Dover in the early seventeenth century. They featured wrestling, dancing, smock races and backsword play. After running for around two hundred years the strain of large crowds, rowdiness and gambling caused their demise in the nineteenth century.

Bowls was a popular peoples' sport despite attempts to restrict its playing. An act passed in 1541 barred bowls for commoners, while allowing it for noblemen. Commoners were ordered to practise archery to boost the military power of the state. The act remained on the statute books until 1845. The phrase bowling alley originates from the use of high hedges to conceal sites for illegal games.

In the seventeenth century the rise of the Puritan movement was to pose greater challenge to popular leisure. The Puritan religious fundamentalism was bringing them into opposition with both the Crown and with popular activities. They were attempting to prevent physical activity and public gatherings on Sundays, which they felt should be devoted to religion.

Under increasing pressure, from the Puritans on the one hand and anti-Puritan elements on the other, King James I was presented with a petition protesting that the lower classes were being prevented from dancing and playing on Sundays after church.

He responded by issuing the 1618 Declaration of Sports. This reasserted traditional rights and customs and the right of people to Sunday recreation. For the first, and really the only time to date, sport and leisure was a major political issue.

Continuing pressure forced King Charles I to re-issue the Declaration in 1633, but the days of his reign were numbered. The brief period of Puritan power between 1640 and 1660 saw a major clampdown on popular recreation. The Puritans attacked dancing for its carnality, football for its violence, maypoles for their paganism and sport in general for despoiling the Sabbath. They suppressed any sport which, like football, could be used to gather a crowd for seditious purposes and outlawed horse-racing, cock-fighting and bear-baiting.

These strictures had much more effect on the common people than on country gentlemen who were able to continue sports debarred to others in the privacy of their own grounds. It is suggested that it was during this period that the lower-class sport of cricket was first taken up by the gentry. But popular sporting traditions often had deep communal roots and persisted through the repression to flourish again with the restoration of the monarchy in 1660.

A more serious threat to the pattern of popular recreations and festivals was posed by the long-term changes in the economic organisation of the countryside. The enclosure of common land, the growth of towns and the beginning of the transition to industrialisation caused a slow but drastic undermining of rural traditions. Traditional playing areas were swallowed up by enclosure, workers were forced off the land and into the towns and there were consequent upheavals in community and tradition.

The survival of popular recreations in the eighteenth century came to depend increasingly upon the patronage of the local gentry. The involvement of the local gentry was a combination of paternalism and self-interest. The provision of festivals which permitted drunkenness and sexual licence was seen by the gentry as a safety valve and a form of social control. The great involvement of the gentry in betting led them to support sports like pedestrianism, which often featured races between the footmen of rival gentry.

There was also a certain amount of political patronage of popular pastimes. The wider franchise meant election contests were now often accompanied by sports and festivities laid on by rival parties in an attempt to outdo each other.

Festivals could, however, also be used for expressions of hostility to authority and often featured mock mayoral ceremonies in which the authorities were parodied. The person chosen as mock mayor was often a drunk or half-wit. He would be paraded around the area making speeches promising full employment, better wages and free beer.

The popular festivals of pre-industrial times were complex occasions. They were neither simply expressions of resistance nor means of social control. In their existing form they were threatened by the social transformation of industrial capitalism.

Many of the features of present-day sport begin to make their first appearance from the early eighteenth century. The developing commercialisation, growth in spectators, offering of prizes, gambling on the result, emergence of professionalism and the development of a degree of spectacle and sensation were all features of the period.

All work and no play

From the middle of the eighteenth century the rise of industrial capitalism began to transform patterns of social life. The traditional forms of popular leisure were to be increasingly undermined over the next hundred years.

The long process of enclosure and rural depopulation was already leading to the decline of the old rural festivals. The festivals and feast days of the new fast-growing towns were to be progressively squeezed out by the rise of capitalism.

The new urban working class found its leisure restricted in three ways. There was no space, there was no time and there was a powerful new ideology that disapproved of physical leisure for the working class.

The new towns grew rapidly. Row upon row of tiny terraced houses sprang up unencumbered by civic regulation or concern about the environment. Very little provision was made for public open space in working-class areas.

Capitalism brought a heightened rate of exploitation. Twelve- and fourteen-hour days, six days a week, left workers too tired for anything else but sleep. Public holidays were drastically cut back. In 1761 there were 47, and in 1825 40. By 1834 there were just four. Many of the traditional occasions for popular celebration had been eliminated.

Popular recreation, undermined in the towns by lack of space and time, was also the subject of attack from a new set of dominant ideas. The Puritan tradition bore fruit in the form of the capitalist work ethic.

Previous attitudes had accepted the place of leisure and popular festival, if only as a safety valve or form of social control. The work ethic represented work as a virtue, idleness as a vice and physical recreation as a hindrance to study and productive labour. Amongst the bourgeoisie there was a developing hostility to the very idea of free time for the labouring classes. There were attempts to regulate leisure and keep holidays to a minimum. Calls were made for tougher laws and magistrates and for the establishment of a police force.

This new attack on the people's leisure was reinforced with the authority of religion. The only free time available to working-class men was Sunday. Women, with their responsibility for domestic labour, could not even enjoy this brief respite. The evangelical movement, however, continued the Puritan hostility to pleasure and recreation on the Sabbath by working to restrict greatly the range of activities that were permitted or socially acceptable.

The campaign against cruel sports reached its peak in the early nineteenth century. Even this movement, which clearly had a progressive side, was primarily an attack on the leisure activities of common people. The 1835 Cruelty to Animals Act outlawed bull- and bear-baiting. Field sports like hunting and shooting remained perfectly acceptable.

Indeed the devotion of the aristocracy to their own particular forms of brutality was at a peak. They fought a constant battle to keep 'their' animals from the hands of poachers and trespassers. In this they had much assistance from the law. The use of automatic spring guns to shoot poachers was perfectly legal until 1827. Even after this date poachers could be transported for a third offence. During the early part of the nineteenth century offences under the game laws accounted for a third of all crime.

Renewed attempts were made to suppress popular sports like football and boxing. The evangelical movement continued its hostility to wakes and festivals and particularly to the outrageous spectacle of men and women dancing. The first half of the nineteenth century greatly heightened the distinction between the old aristocracy free to enjoy their sporting pursuits, a new bourgeoisie committed to the single-minded pursuit of profit and the working classes who must be protected from the temptations of leisure and pleasure.

The public schools and the Oxbridge blues

While the proletariat worked and the aristocracy played, a new cult was developing in the public schools of the mid-nineteenth century – the cult of athleticism. A fanatical devotion to sport, and in particular to team games, at public school and university was the crucible that eventually produced the formation of organised sporting institutions in the last quarter of the nineteenth century.

The roots of this fanaticism for games lay in the reorganisation of the public schools in the 1840s. By this point the schools had become somewhat anarchic. Indicative of a peculiar combination of self-reliance and internal hierarchy, there was a large degree of self-government by boys, based on prefects and the fagging system. There were elements of a stress on team spirit – an emphasis on group loyalty, conformity and herd instinct – but the traditional pastimes of the aristocratic pupil were, with the exception of cricket, rather individual. Boating, hunting and riding were all popular.

There was increasing concern about the degree of anarchy prevailing, the lack of control staff had over pupils and the extensive gambling, cruelty and 'immorality'.

But the schools were beginning to change with the full development of the Victorian middle class. This new wealthy bourgeoisie was anxious to gain social status for its male children through the public schools and it was these children who were to become the most enthusiastic devotees of the new cult for games.

Team games were seen as a way of establishing greater social control over the boys' leisure time and also as a means of draining off excess energy and therefore repressing manifestations of developing sexuality. These games were at first introduced only reluctantly by staff but their popularity with the pupils and value in maintaining discipline soon secured them a central place in the curriculum.

A government enquiry into the public schools, the Clarendon Commission of 1861, recognised the value of games for 'character training' and saw cricket and football not just as means of exercise and amusement but also as ways of forming some of the most durable qualities and manly virtues. Games were also seen as a way of preventing immorality, by which they meant homosexuality and masturbation.

The concepts of sport as a form of social control, as a way of developing character, as a way of defining masculinity and as a way of repressing sexuality have all left a deep mark on English sport.

The 1860s saw the emergence of the games master and the development of inter-house competition, soon followed by competition between schools. The cult became self-sustaining. Public school games players went on to be university games players and then often returned to teaching, where they played their part in popularising sport, influencing a whole new generation of pupils.

This was a time of expansion in the number of public schools and recruitment became important. Extensive facilities for games became an important point of appeal to parents and much money was spent on acquiring and developing playing fields.

Games were rapidly becoming more important than study in the schools and it was in this period that the distinction between the sporting philistine and the non-sporting aesthete became marked. There was a growing suspicion of excessive intellectualism and an interest in culture and the arts became regarded as effeminate and unmanly by many in the public school world. Only the games player was truly masculine.

The public school ethos under late Victorian capitalism was an odd amalgam. A tradition of Christian gentility combined with a sport-based concept of masculinity, and a belief that Darwin's 'survival of the fittest' principle applied to the social life as well as to the animal world. An emphasis on success, aggression, ruthlessness and the need for leadership combined with an altruistic courtesy in triumph, compassion to the defeated and stress upon fair play.

The public school system had become an important part of the imperialist system as a whole, producing an officer class to rule the empire. Having been schooled in the virtues of sport for instilling discipline and team work, this officer class then spread English team sport, particularly cricket and rugger, throughout the empire.

But as well as an officer class, sent off into the empire convinced of the white man's right to rule, the public schools also produced the muscular Christians, who combined religion and sport, seeing the latter as a way of promoting the Christian ethos. They set out into the world convinced of the importance of sport and the need to spread its values amongst the lower orders. The association of sport and Christianity in this period was strong. During Victoria's reign, of 695 Oxbridge cricket blues, no fewer than 295 became Anglican clergymen. The muscular Christians were influential in the formation of many English football clubs, and in the development of cricket in the late nineteenth century.

Gentlemen and players

This section outlines the formation of the principal institutions of English sport in the last quarter of the nineteenth century. It was the period that saw the domination of sport by a class and by a gender – the men of the Victorian bourgeoisie – enshrined in organisational form. The great myth of English sport is that it was all dreamed up by Victorian gentlemen, drawing upon the noble amateur traditions of ancient Greece. There is very little truth in this notion and it serves only to confuse.

England's major sports, athletics, football, cricket, golf, racing and even tennis, were all around in one form or another long before the late nineteenth century. Most of these sports had been engaged in at one time or another by both the upper and the lower classes.

There was nothing very noble about the sports of ancient Greece. They were not specifically for the amateur – the Greeks made no distinction between paid and unpaid and many winners received substantial material rewards. They did not believe taking part to be more important than winning. The Greek games excluded women and slaves.

The distinction between the amateur and the professional, such a strong feature of English sport, was basically a Victorian creation and is little more than class distinction in disguised form.

The term amateur came originally from early eighteenth-century France, where it meant a connoisseur of the fine arts. By the end of the century it referred to the so-called 'polite' arts of painting and music. By the mid-nineteenth century it was used more broadly to refer to gentlemen of leisure and taste – an amateur was a gentleman. It was in this form that the term first became widely applied in relation to sport.

The growth in public school and university sport and the formation of sport clubs were boosting the extent to which people were prepared to travel for competition. The growth of the railways from the 1840s transformed the nature of sporting competition. Matches between teams from different towns and different regions became much more feasible.

But this gave rise to problems over rules. Different areas had evolved different variants of the same game. The need for standardisation emerged first in public school and inter-varsity sport. Standardisation required agreement over rules. But determining agreed rules could not be separated from the social authority to enforce them. It was the men of the public school and university world who, by virtue of their social power and influence, became the prominent figures in the formation of sport institutions.

At this point a distinction should be made. There was a whole set of sports such as athletics, football and rugby, whose governing bodies were formed between 1870 and 1900. In these sports the men of the Victorian bourgeoisie played a dominant role in the foundation of institutions. But some sports such as cricket, golf and racing had already established institutions. The Royal and Ancient Golf Club, the Jockey Club and the Marylebone Cricket Club were all creations of the eighteenth century in which the traditional aristocracy played a greater role.

The most distinctive feature of the Victorian developments was the establishment of rigid distinctions between the professional and the amateur. The word amateur was first applied to sport in mid-nineteenth-century rowing. It referred to anyone who was not a waterman or otherwise employed on the water. But it soon became clear that it really referred to gentlemen as opposed to workers.

The word was taken up by the Amateur Athletic Club in 1867. Its rules excluded from membership anyone who was a mechanic, an artisan or a labourer. This became a point of conflict within athletics and in sport generally. Battles over who could and could not compete, and to what extent payment should be allowed to compensate for lost earnings while playing sport, were prominent for the next 30 years.

The battle over the amateur/professional distinction was in reality a displaced form of class tension. Almost every sport had to find a way of handling it. Cricket and golf developed separate classes of player: the gentleman and the player, the full member and the artisan. Rugby split into two separate games, while football retained professional and amateur games under the same overall authority. Athletics, swimming and tennis simply outlawed professionalism entirely. Examining this period when institutions were formed and power consolidated reveals much about the variations between England's main sports.

Athletics played a key role in the development of amateurism. Various forms of athletics had existed for several centuries. The rural festivities of the sixteenth and seventeenth centuries featured running races. A tradition of rural athletic meetings in the eighteenth century became particularly strong in the north of England and Scotland with events like the Highland Games and the Border

Games. Pedestrianism and the running of head-to-head matches for gambling was well established before the nineteenth century. In the nineteenth century it is known that there were both open professional athletics events, with prizes, and open meetings that were mainly middle-class affairs, with low-value prizes.

The amateur concept arrived with public school and Oxbridge participation. A three-way battle developed over the Amateur Athletic Club's controversially explicit exclusion of mechanics, labourers and artisans. The London Athletic Club, which was building a broader lower-middle-class base, was challenging the AAC power over athletics. During the 1870s more working-class-oriented organisations began to emerge in the north.

With chaos threatening, three Oxbridge men intervened. The social authority they were a part of enabled them to engineer a compromise. In 1880 the Amateur Athletic Association was formed. The barring of mechanic, artisan and labourer was dropped, but the distinction between amateur and professional became absolute. To compete for money put one forever outside the world of organised athletics.

The enshrinement of the distinction between the amateur and the professional meant that gentlemen of leisure had a huge and permanent advantage over those whose work left little time for training and preparation. This proscription of the paid athlete was written into the constitution of sport after sport.

Football handled the class tension in a rather different manner. As a pre-industrial game it had a long chequered history, involving outbreaks of violence, attempts at suppression and the use of matches as a pretext for political agitation. It was more distinctly a people's game in that it never attracted much interest or patronage from the aristocracy.

It was traditionally played in informal circumstances with mass participation, few clear rules, vast playing areas, very long games and an absence of referees. This form of football effectively began to die out with the rise of industrialisation, the enclosure of common land and the drift to the towns.

While the new urban working class had neither the time nor the space for football, it was taken up by the public schools, where the first attempts to evolve an agreed set of rules took place. Several different forms of the game had developed between 1848 and 1863 and there were attempts centring upon Cambridge to formulate an agreed code.

In 1863 the Football Association was formed, largely by ex-public-school men. The FA banned hacking, tripping and running with the ball, which led to the break-away of Blackheath and the emergence of rugby as a distinct game. The amateur dominance of both games was soon challenged by their growing working-class following. Each sport responded differently.

When football emerged from the public schools in its new codified form it rapidly became a highly popular working-class game. While many famous football clubs emerged from institutions like churches and schools, many others grew out of the workplace. Stoke City, Crewe Alexandra and Manchester United were all formed by groups of railway workers. Coventry City emerged from Singer's sewing machine factory, West Ham United from Thames Ironworks, and Arsenal from the Woolwich munitions factory.

For its first eleven years from 1872 the FA Cup was dominated by the public school teams. But football was growing rapidly in the industrial midlands and north. It was attracting a large working-class audience and the income from spectators made it possible for the clubs to attract talented players with payments – illegal under the FA rules.

Attempts to prevent the development of professionalism were unsuccessful and a showdown came in 1884 with the threat led by Preston to form a break-away organisation. Rather than lose their monopoly control, the FA decided to allow a limited degree of professionalism.

In 1888 the Football League, based on twelve clubs in the midlands and north, was formed. The rise of working-class football contributed to a gradual decline of middle-class interest, and the eclipse of public school teams in the FA Cup after 1882 led to the FA launching a separate cup competition restricted to amateur teams ten years later in 1892.

The FA remained the supreme governing body of football but the greater working-class popularity of the game and the compromise with the league over professionalism meant that its control was less total than that of the AAA over athletics. The Football League and the clubs, however, were not controlled by the working class but predominantly by the industrial bourgeoisie.

Most professional clubs had had humble origins but the financial base of the game was transformed by football's development as a spectator sport. Professional players were hired, stadiums were developed and the game rapidly became organised along business lines. By the end of the century the majority of clubs had become limited companies owned by their shareholders and controlled by boards of directors.

The emergence of professionalism in rugby was handled very differently. Like football, rugby grew rapidly in popularity. The Rugby Football Union was formed in 1871 in a Pall Mall restaurant by 32 clubs. By 1893 there were 481.

The popularity of the game amongst the working class in Lancashire and Yorkshire led, as in football, to demands that players be compensated for lost earnings. This demand for broken time payments caused a showdown and in 1895 the northern clubs broke away to form the Northern Union, which in 1922 became the Rugby League.

Initially the Northern Union was by no means in favour of complete professionalism. They insisted that players have a job outside rugby as the sport was supposed to be only a pastime, with no real financial reward.

The split, which led to the development of two distinctly different games, was to cause a class polarisation. Rugby League remained restricted largely to the north and became as deep-rooted a working-class game as football. Rugby Union became, except in Wales, a sport largely based upon public schools, grammar schools, universities, and old boys' associations. It gradually replaced football as a public school sport, as football became increasingly identified with professionalism and with the proletariat.

At the outbreak of the first world war rugby union games were suspended but football continued. Even though football games were used for large-scale recruitment into the imperial army, it became seen by the upper classes as an unpatriotic sport and its social status within the public school world was further diminished.

Sports like football, rugby and athletics acquired governing bodies only in the late nineteenth century. Other sports, such as cricket, golf and racing, had established institutions in the eighteenth century. But these sports were also to be transformed in the period 1875–1900.

Cricket's supreme authoritative body, the MCC, dates back to 1787. But its control was relatively informal and undefined and the organisation of cricket as we know it today was as much a product of the late Victorian era.

Cricket in one form or another had a long history as an informal folk game before being taken up by the aristocracy during the seventeenth century. This had two consequences. First, there was a growth in various forms of rural cricket under aristocratic patronage. Second, cricket became the subject of extensive gambling. The MCC emerged in the eighteenth century as an offshoot of an exclusive gentlemen's club, but cricket continued to be played in a variety of forms, from country houses to village greens.

The importance of gambling contributed to the emergence of the first professionals. Upper-class men became keen to boost the chances of their teams by employing talented players.

These cricket professionals were often retained by gentlemen's cricket clubs. As well as providing talent for the club side in competition they were also expected to be on hand to bowl at the members in the nets whenever required.

The growth of this possibility of employment in cricket was extended with the emergence in the nineteenth century of a professional touring team. William Clarke's All-England Eleven brought together some of the best professional cricketers and travelled the country playing local sides. Cricket was developing as a spectator sport and beginning to change from a pursuit of the gentry to a national game.

The rise of the Victorian bourgeoisie produced a new stratum of country gentleman whose influence on cricket gradually became greater. As in other sports there was a new concern to mark clearly the distinction between the classes. The new county clubs were gradually coming to occupy a central place in the cricketing world. They occupied the middle ground between the populist travelling teams and the elitist country house game. As public interest switched from the touring professional circuses to the new county game, professionals had to come to terms with their new employers. In the last quarter of the century, as the County Championship developed, the authority of the amateur gentlemen over cricket was consolidated.

In this period, the conventions of separating gentlemen and 'players', i.e. professionals, grew into formal rigidity. Amateurs had their own dressing rooms, ate separately and entered grounds by their own gates. Their initials came before their surnames on scorecards, whereas professionals' initials came after. Professionals not only had to bowl at club members in the nets, they also had to help roll out the wicket.

Athletics outlawed the professionals and rugby split into two separate games, but cricket contrived to create an internal caste system, echoing the class divisions of society as a whole.

Golf, in its early pre-seventeenth-century forms, was played by all classes of society, by men and women, mainly on the north-east coast of Scotland. During the eighteenth century segregation between three classes of players began to develop. These were the gentlemen of leisure, the artisans and traders, and the professionals – mainly club and ball makers.

The development of competition required an agreed set of rules. The Royal and Ancient Club of St Andrews, another exclusive club, gradually became, like the MCC for cricket and the Jockey Club for racing, the recognised authority. At this stage golf was still played on common land and the courses, unlike the clubs, were accessible to all.

During the nineteenth century the game spread to England and was taken up increasingly by the middle and upper classes. Tension between the various users of common land grew and the growth of private courses began. The new suburban middle classes were well placed to buy up the large tracts of land required for private golf clubs. Social exclusivity became an important part of the game's appeal. High subscription fees and vetting of potential members kept out the working class.

Some clubs did introduce special category membership for artisans. In exchange for limited access to the course, at hours not popular with full members, artisan members were expected to tend the grounds. They were given wooden huts, carefully hidden away from the opulent club houses that the full members enjoyed. In Scotland golf retained some of its working-class following and courses such as St Andrews, owned by the town, remained open to all. But golf in England rapidly became a badge of social status and a means of making and sustaining business contracts.

As in cricket, clubs employed professionals to teach the game to their members. Golf professionals were given the rights to make money selling equipment in the club shop. Socially, however, this marked them as traders, inferior to the club members, and they were treated as such.

Even *boxing*, for a long time the prerogative of lower-class boxers, patronised by the aristocracy, became subject to the reorganising influence of the Victorian bourgeoisie. After a peak of popularity between 1800 and 1825 prize-fighting had been successfully outlawed. Its revival after 1867 was another product of public school and university enthusiasm for sport. The famous Queensberry Rules were in fact drawn up not by the Marquis of Queensberry but by a fellow student, John Chambers. The Marquis was approached to sponsor the rules to ensure their success.

Chambers himself was a key figure in the university dominance of sport organisation. As well as devising the Queensberry Rules he rowed in and coached Cambridge boat race teams, staged a Cup Final, and started championships for athletics, cycling, boxing, billiards and wrestling.

The universities and public schools produced in the late nineteenth century a generation of men who played a dominant part in forming the institutions of many sports. But another important source of sport organisation was suburban life.

The rapid growth of the cities had led to the development of areas of suburban housing for the affluent upper-middle class. This class developed distinctive forms of leisure. They played an important part in the growth of golf clubs and took up the newer game of tennis with great enthusiasm.

The game of Real (or Royal) *tennis* had been popular with the court in the sixteenth century but had virtually died out by the Industrial Revolution. The new game of lawn tennis that developed in the 1870s was a reworked combination of real tennis, rackets and other bat and ball games. It rapidly supplanted croquet as the game to be played on middle-class lawns after lunch. The MCC had some early involvement in forming rules but lawn tennis was soon adopted by the All-England Croquet Club.

After the first Wimbledon Championships of 1877, tennis rapidly became the major area of activity and the club changed its name to the All-England Lawn Tennis and Croquet Club in 1884. This club has retained great exclusivity. Together with the Lawn Tennis Association it dominates English tennis, which has consequently become another sport played by all classes but ruled by one.

Racing is another sport in which class relations were firmly inscribed at an early stage. British racing is ruled by the Jockey Club, one of the most exclusive clubs in the country. This self-electing elite of 110 men, answerable to no one, wields absolute power over racing. It controls the activities of trainers and jockeys and operates the system of stewards' enquiries. In the fifteen hundred enquiries held each year, penalties can range from fines and suspensions to the ultimate power to warn off for life – that is, to bar someone permanently from all race tracks.

The most distinctive feature about the ruling of most English sport, however, is the use of a distinction between the amateur and the professional as a means of consolidating class power. The explicit exclusion of artisans in rowing persisted well into the twentieth century. The 1936 Australian Olympic Games team were excluded from Henley because they were policemen and hence artisans. Rugby Union developed 17 pages of stringent rules about amateur status, in which Rugby League players are totally excluded from Rugby Union, even if they are unpaid Rugby League players.

Women, of all classes, encountered a far greater barrier to full involvement in sport than did working-class men. English sport is one of the most distinctly male of all social institutions. Sport has been played more by men, watched more by men, and, crucially, controlled by men. It plays a significant part in the whole cultural image of masculinity.

This is not a product of the nature of sport. It is part of a more general pattern in which social power is exerted by men over women. It is also a very specific product of the all-male upper- and middle-class world of the public schools and universities.

The key institutions of sport emerged from this all-male world. Just as their organisational rules and underlying assumptions enshrined class dominance, so they also enshrined gender dominance in a lasting structured form.

Women of all classes were distanced from the world of sport, but in rather different ways. The middle of the nineteenth century was a period when leisure for working people was severely limited. But when the struggle of organised labour for shorter hours began to bear fruit after 1860 it was mainly men who benefited.

The responsibility placed on women for domestic labour meant that less paid work time in the factory merely made for more unpaid work time in the home. Middle-class women enjoyed the leisure particular to those classes who could afford to employ domestic staff. However, the Victorian conventions held that women were frail, should behave in a ladylike manner and refrain from strenuous physical exercise. Women of the aristocracy were never so confined by the codes of Victorian gentility and had more access to and involvement in sporting pursuits. However, the sporting pursuits of the aristocracy were still very much their traditional pastimes, riding and the other equestrian sports, and the various form of animal slaughter we call field sports.

For women who were able to overcome the obstacles to involvement in sport in the nineteenth century the next barrier was dress. The conventions of dress carried over on to the sports field. Long heavy skirts were the accepted wear for golf and hockey right into the twentieth century. Tennis was played in tight skirts with trains.

The development of women's tees, nearer the hole, in golf was not simply an attempt to mark women's supposed lesser strength. It was also an attempt to discourage women from making full swings, which were seen as unladylike and inconsistent with the accepted full-skirted dress.

There is a great irony here. The development of that symbol of masculine aggression, overarm bowling, has been widely attributed to women cricketers – the full skirts they wore made the conventional underarm bowling difficult.

The Rational Dress Society fought for more sensible clothing for women, both for sport and for everyday life. They commented in 1887 that the present style of dress made it impossible for women to walk properly. Their efforts were boosted by the spread of cycling as a popular pastime between 1890 and 1914. The popularity of cycling with women led to forms of dress that were less physically restricting.

Early attempts to develop physical education for women had to struggle against unsuitable conventions of dress. The Bergmann Osterberg Physical Training College pioneered women's physical education in this country. They developed the gym tunic and forbade corsets but had only partial success in changing accepted sporting dress. In 1912 the England hockey captain was ordered to lengthen her skirt. Ladylike respectability was still more important than freedom of movement.

Real changes in women's sporting dress did not come until after the first world war. The breakdown of Edwardian respectability and a transformation of social manners and morals meant women's clothes generally changed. In sport the popular successes of the athletic tennis star Suzanne Lenglen had a major influence. Her skirt, reaching just below the knee, was considered daring, but it soon became the accepted form of dress for tennis and ankle-length skirts became a thing of the past.

Suzanne Lenglen is recalled in traditional histories more for this revolution in dress than for her tennis success. This is typical of the treatment of women's sport as peripheral and trivial.

Unsuitable dress was only the first obstacle. A larger problem was presented by male control of almost all sport institutions and the dominant feeling within these institutions was that women's sport was not something to be encouraged. The AAA was and is men only and wanted nothing to do with women's athletics. It was only in 1922 that a Women's Amateur Athletic Association was formed. The Baron de Coubertin, one of the founders of the modern Olympic Games, was shocked by the sight of lightly clad women engaged in strenuous activity. He felt their only role should be to crown the winner.

Women were not allowed to compete in the Olympics until 1928. But the sight of exhausted women crossing the line at the end of the 800 metres was too much for the sensitive male souls of the IOC. Women were not allowed to run this length again until 1960.

Despite the many barriers women did achieve success in the early days of sport, even though their achievements were often hidden from history. One of the first famous woman athletes was tennis player Lottie Dods. She introduced speed, attacking net play and the smash to women's tennis. She first won Wimbledon in 1887 when she was 15 and won it four more times in the next six years. She never lost at Wimbledon and is believed to have lost only four matches in her entire tennis career.

At 21 she gave up tennis for golf and won the English championships. She was a first-class archer, an international hockey player and also an ice skater. However, despite such achievements women's sport was still generally treated by the governing bodies and the press as a diversion, an inferior imitation of the real thing.

This chapter has outlined the way in which the institutions of sport were formed. The crucial feature was the rise of the bourgeoisie to a position of social authority in the nineteenth century. In the world of sport this enabled it to assume positions of power and influence in the governing bodies of most major sports.

The rigid distinctions erected between the amateur and the professional were in the end rooted in class domination. The formation of these institutions on the base of public school and university sport made them also an expression of the domination of social life by men. This does not mean than no women or working-class people were involved in sport during this period. But such involvement was always within the bounds of authority exercised by the men of the bourgeoisie.

4.

Playing under Capitalism

In the last 60 years sport has grown into an international spectacle and a multi-million-pound business. This chapter examines the growth of that spectacle, the degree to which dominant sporting values have been resisted and the continuing resilience of popular forms of recreation.

The first section traces the emergence of spectator sport and the growth of spectacle. The spreading of television to almost every home and the consequent economic transformation of sport by sponsorship is a central part of the process.

The second section examines different ways in which the power of the dominant authorities to define and control sport has been challenged. Labour relations, the workers' sport movements of the inter-war years, and women's sport can all be seen as attempts to challenge dominant assumptions, not always successfully.

The final section looks more closely at forms of popular recreation. Shaped as they are by the leisure industry, available facilities, accepted conventions of behaviour and by people's attempts to shape and control, within very different limits, their own lives, forms of popular recreation are bound to be contradictory.

Spectacle

Spectator sport
Between 1880 and 1939 sports rapidly developed as spectator sports with large popular appeal. The foundations of the mass spectacle, which has become the focus of much television coverage, were laid. The crowd appeal of many sports was realised and the process of paying admission formalised.

With the growth of regular competition a fixture list was assured and the habit of spectatorship given a structure. The distinct separation of players and supporters helped give rise to a whole new culture surrounding sport – a fan culture in which stars developed. The emergence of a large-scale mass-circulation popular press, the spread of comics, the growth of working-class literacy and the later emergence of broadcasting all contributed to this emergent sporting culture. Massively supported rituals like the Cup Final became firmly established in public life.

Once national sport was established, international sport soon began to develop. The first modern Olympics had been held in 1896 but the real basis for international competition was laid in the twentieth century. By 1915 international bodies had been established for cricket, football, tennis and athletics.

Sport spread out along the network of empire. International sport developed almost as a form of diplomacy, maintaining contact with friendly nations. It soon became a symbol of national virility to be successful at sport.

Spectating was not a new phenomenon. There had been a long tradition of large crowds gathering for sporting events before the 1880s. In the eighteenth century crowds of up to ten thousand were known to watch cricket at the Artillery grounds in Finsbury Park and crowds of twenty thousand had been drawn to the Cotswold Games. In the early part of the nineteenth century, prize-fighting could draw twenty thousand people to bouts. Pedestrianism was regularly watched by ten thousand or more. Racing, too, was popular. In 1824 seventeen thousand paid to see a game of cricket at Sheffield.

But it was only towards the end of the nineteenth century, after the formation of sport institutions, the inauguration of nationally based competitions and the establishment of fixture lists, that spectator sport became an organised and regular feature of social life. The Football Association Cup Final, started in 1872, was watched by two thousand. By 1893 the crowd was forty-five thousand and by 1913 a phenomenal one hundred and twenty thousand crowded into Crystal Palace to see the match. From 1923 the competition found its permanent home at Wembley and an annual crowd of one hundred thousand. (In the first famous Wembley final, over twice this many gained entry, many by climbing the walls.)

Cricket's County Championship began in 1873 and after reorganisation in 1895 built its own regular audience. Athletics was slower to develop but began a boom after the first world war with crowds of thirty thousand for the AAA Championships, in those days held at Stamford Bridge.

The inter-war period saw the emergence of new sports and the continued popularity of older ones. The popularity of the athletic French tennis player, Suzanne Lenglen, contributed to a growth in women's sport. Rowing, cycling, swimming and running were taken up by women in greater numbers.

Gambling was becoming a major feature of working-class life, in increasingly organised forms. The popularity of horse-racing was supplemented by the introduction of greyhound-racing in the 1920s and the massive growth of football pools in the 1930s.

The Betting Act of 1928 introduced the Racecourse Betting Control Board and the Totalisator. In the following year £230 million was gambled on the horses, not including the incalculable millions that changed hands in illegal off-course betting. Greyhound-racing was introduced in 1926 and by 1932 there were 187 tracks with annual attendances of around eighteen million.

Motorised sports introduced before the first world war continued to develop, although participation was largely restricted to the socially privileged. Dirt-track motor-bike racing was introduced from the USA in the 1920s and soon won a large working-class following.

Along with the growth in spectatorship went the development of a culture of sport on a large scale. The growth of the distinction between spectators and players and the development of full-time sport, whether played by professionals or amateurs, encouraged the emergence of star teams and individuals. The popular press, particularly after the first world war, began to devote increasing space to sport.

When the BBC became a public corporation in 1927 it began to broadcast running commentaries on sporting events. For the first time major occasions like Cup Finals and test matches, and the exploits of star names who played in them, were relayed direct into the home. A whole range of comics and specialist magazines helped foster the growth of stardom as did the massively popular cigarette cards. Top sports people were household names as never before.

Sport, in becoming successful, had adopted regular formats, rationalised its organisation, evolved a form of division of labour and a dependence upon cash flow. In short, it had many of the features of any capitalist enterprise. Yet for the most part it was still organised as if it was a hobby. Athletics was run largely by spare-time voluntary effort. Tennis, cricket and golf were all based largely upon networks of membership clubs.

Even football, that most successful of sporting enterprises, was not really run as a conventional business. Only the larger and more successful clubs had any real profit potential. There was a constant pressure for reinvestment not just in ground facilities but in that most intangible of assets, playing staff. Restrictions were imposed by the Football League on the payment of dividends to shareholders. Crucially the structure of football club ownership had not grown primarily out of the desire for profits. Football club owners were more interested in power and prestige in the community. Football was a way of becoming known and sustaining business contacts. Added to this was the desire to pursue schoolboy hobbies into adulthood.

English sport in general was dominated by a form of part-time amateur paternalism. This form of organisation was not without some positive features, despite its general anti-democratic character.

It did ensure that money remained within sport rather than being reinvested outside it. This was important as the financial base of even the most popular sports had always been insecure. The governing bodies of many sports had mechanisms by which finance was diverted to the more impoverished parts of the game.

The Football League system, for example, takes a levy of all gate money which is then distributed amongst the 92 clubs. In effect this means money goes from the more successful first-division clubs to support the others. The main merit of this system is that it sustains and subsidises first-class football in areas that otherwise could not support a league team. Similarly the small clubs in many sports have depended upon money being diverted to them from more successful ventures. The power of governing authorities of sports has in the past meant that limited financial resources can be shared out fairly, although this is not always done.

This form of paternalist voluntary organisation was to become increasingly vulnerable after the second world war. The rise of television turned sport into a whole new cultural form, with extensive marketing potential. Yet this process happened as sport itself was coming under increasing financial pressure. In the last 20 years the allied force of television and sponsorship has transformed sport and in the process undermined the lower of its traditional authorities.

Armchair viewing

Sport has always occupied an important space within the world of television. The BBC in particular has prided itself on its sports coverage, which provides an important element of its corporate prestige. Sport reaches a much greater audience via the screen that it ever has reached in the stadium. Nowadays, for most people most of the time, sport means television sport.

The beginnings were slow. Britain's television service was fully launched in 1946. The pre-war experiments with television never reached more than about twenty thousand sets. After the war the cost of sets was still high, and in the period of post-war austerity people were reluctant to buy them. Even by 1950 the new television service was still reaching only 340,000 homes. In the early 1950s, however, the growth in people's disposable income boosted set sales and by 1954 television had reached 3,250,000.

The arrival of commercial television in 1955 gave another impetus. The BBC was given a second channel in 1964 and both BBC and ITV introduced colour in the late 1960s. By 1968 over 90 per cent of homes had television. In 20 years television had gone from being the luxury commodity of a small elite to being the principal leisure activity for most of the population.

Sport had been important to the BBC even in pre-television days. Radio commentaries brought sporting events into the home. The prominence of events like the Cup Final, the Boat Race, Wimbledon, the test matches and Rugby Union internationals had been enhanced by the attention given to them by the BBC.

Television soon gave sport the same degree of attention. Sport offered a source of programming that was potentially both cheap and popular. In the late 1940s the BBC succeeded in getting coverage of many events simply by paying a facility fee of £25. Even by 1952 few events cost the BBC more than £250 to obtain. Sport authorities spent a lot of time worrying about the possible adverse effect of television coverage on live attendances and were slow to see the financial possibilities of television fees.

The imminent arrival of ITV was not taken seriously in many parts of the BBC, whose attitude was one of aloof superiority. The Outside Broadcast department were rather more alive to the threat of competition. Fees rose as the BBC set about securing their sport coverage by signing long-term agreements with a number of sport organisations.

So ITV started with a number of disadvantages. The BBC had the contacts, the contracts and the technical expertise. ITV's system of separate regional companies meant that no single company could maintain extensive outside broadcast facilities. Co-ordination was hampered by the lukewarm attitude of some ITV chiefs to the audience potential of sport.

For many years the BBC held the initiative, even though ITV did compete over Wimbledon coverage with some success in the late 1950s. The BBC's dominance was reinforced by a government agreement that neither channel could obtain an exclusive coverage of six so-called 'national' events (the Cup Final, Wimbledon tennis, the Boat Race, the Derby, the Grand National and test matches). It was hard for ITV, hampered by regular ad breaks, to win audiences if both channels showed an event. The ITV companies soon realised that, with the exception of the Cup Final, if they could not have an exclusive deal the events were not worth covering.

The gaining of a second channel gave the BBC an even greater advantage, enabling it to cover Wimbledon and test matches from start to finish. Sport was finding its fixed places on Saturday afternoon and Wednesday night. Regular Saturday night football soon became popular.

Sport, however, occupies an unusual place in the television schedules. While sport is quite popular it is rarely popular enough to be scheduled at peak viewing times. This is partly because it is less successful than other types of programme in gaining women viewers. So the regular sport programmes, *Grandstand* and *World of Sport*, *Sportsnight* and *Midweek Sport Special*, *Match of The Day*, *The Big Match* and the other football programmes, are all outside, or at best on the edge of, peak viewing time.

But the picture is transformed at times of major events. The World Cup, the Olympic Games and the World Snooker Championships have an almost unique ability to win and hold huge audiences. These events also have a totally unique ability to hold large audiences at off-peak hours or late at night. So, during these major events, the regular schedules are torn apart to make way for liberal doses of sport.

Television has made watching sport a new form of shared national ritual. Over half the country watch the Cup Final. While the 1950s saw the Boat Race, the Cup Final and Wimbledon become national events in a new sense, the 1960s saw the growth of sport as a global spectacle.

Developments in television and satellite technology gradually made it possible to relay an event in any part of the world live to every other part. The Apollo moon shots, American presidential elections, Olympic Games and World Cups have all been beamed around the world.

Football matches in the 1978 Argentine World Cup were timed to fit peak viewing-time television in Europe. Major sport events have become subject to complex financial relations between multinational communications consortia. The development of elaborate television technology has great merits. Watching high-definition colour pictures of a live sporting event can be great fun. Merely adopting an attitude of puritan hostility would be silly. But television undoubtedly produces a very particular way of looking at sport. Because it reaches so many and because, along with sponsorship, it is also of great financial importance to sport, it has changed the nature of sport itself.

Television is, for better or worse, a mass medium. The bulk of its costs are in production rather than distribution. The real expense is in making the programme. Once made, it costs no more to send a programme to forty million people than to forty thousand.

So there are great pressures to maximise the audience. With sport coverage, programme-makers are not primarily worried about sport fans. They will watch anyway. The audience they are most anxious about, most keen to appeal to, is the peripheral one. They want the programmes to appeal to people who are not sport addicts but will watch a sport programme if it promises to be entertaining.

Sport fans also like entertainment, but the traditional characteristic of entertainment in sport is that it is uncertain and unpredictable. No promoter can guarantee an exciting match. The crowd would not expect this. The uncertainty of the entertainment value is what has distinguished sport from show business.

But television needs to minimise this uncertainty. In order to hold the marginal audience it needs to be able to deliver entertainment even if the raw material is not promising. A striking feature of sport coverage is the time devoted to previews, post-mortems, interviews, discussion and action replays, as opposed to direct coverage of the event itself. If the match is bad maybe the amusing banter of the experts can placate us. If there are no goals, they will show us last week's goals again.

Television does not simply relay sport to us. It presents a particular view of sport, framed by its own selection of shots and the addition of its own commentary. It is a particular view, inviting us to look at events in a particular way.

The attempt to reach, through entertainment values, a large audience, means a constant attempt to forge links with that audience, to establish points of identification. So the coverage attempts constantly to engage our involvement in the stories of sport with endless speculation about what might happen and who will win.

The focal point of these stories are the star characters with whom we are instantly familiar, thanks to frequent interviews and close-ups during the action. Our understanding of the action itself is rooted in the star system. The World Cup coverage told us a lot about the stars to look for in the teams of, say, Italy and Brazil. It did very little to explain the differences in style between the two as teams.

Television has constantly to distinguish between sporting events of greater and lesser importance. It has evolved a calendar of major events, repeated year after year, offered to us as the peak moments of the sporting calender. Yet it is a very particular selection. Some events, such as the Boat Race, or Rugby Union internationals, have a prominence much greater than their public following would seem to warrant. Other highly popular sports such as cycling, swimming, netball, speedway and greyhound-racing get very little exposure.

Television's selection is not, however, simply a result of the class background of its producers. The need to develop sports that work as small-screen entertainment is an important pressure. Television turned the obscure upper-class pursuit of show-jumping into a big audience winner. But it has done the same with darts and snooker, more working-class-based sports. Sports like squash and angling, on the other hand, have defied successful television. Television priorities constantly suggest to us that some sports are more important than others.

Men's events are also constantly marked as being more important than women's. In tennis, athletics and swimming it is always the male events that come to occupy the central place. In the few sports where a greater focus is placed upon women, such as gymnastics and skating, television tends to emphasise the supposed 'aesthetic' qualities of grace, poise, elegance and timing. These sports are regarded as more 'feminine' and so women's participation is more acceptable.

Even the values and qualities regarded as important in performers represent a particular way of seeing the world. There is a tendency to lay greater stress on the need for toughness, aggression and courage, as opposed to, say, balance, timing and dexterity.

These attitudes are not peculiar to television. But in constantly relaying and reproducing them television perpetuates dominant gender stereotypes that serve to oppress women.

Television also directs our attention firmly towards British, or ideally English, involvement in sport. National events are given prime importance and victory is treated as a vital matter. Judgements constantly evoke national stereotypes – the Latins are fiery and temperamental, the Germans are efficient but cold and calculating, and so on.

Somehow, though, the other nations never quite manage that perfect blend of skill and commitment captured by the bulldog breed of the Brits. It is our boys (and it usually is boys rather than girls) who are prepared to do it all, run and run and play from the heart. We admire the skills of the French and the Brazilians but when it's backs-to-the-wall time there's no substitute for work-rate.

Television, then, does not simply show sport. It shows it in a particular way. It relates events as stories with star characters. It re-presents sport as spectacular entertainment. The underlying values reproduce stereotypical attitudes of men and women, of Britishness and of foreigners.

Most of us spend a large proportion of our leisure time watching television. Sport coverage occupies as much as a sixth of air time. So the way that television shows sport probably plays a part in shaping the way that we see and understand the world.

It has certainly helped to change the face of sport. This is not simply because it pays money for coverage that most sports are glad to receive. Much larger sums are available in sponsorship money. Companies are keen to sponsor events that are televised. So a whole range of sports have been prepared to change the form of events to make them more attractive to television. The next section will outline the growth of sponsorship.

Pay up and play the game

The post-war period saw a substantial expansion of the leisure industry. Television became universal and the single most popular leisure activity. The record industry launched the long-playing record and the stereo hi-fi became an everyday device. Car ownership rose dramatically and mobility increased. Ordinary working people became able to take holidays abroad. Traditional sports began to lose popularity to newer diversions. Their organisations, dominated by an amateur paternalist approach, were slow to respond and failed to take decisive action. Change has instead been forced on the sports world by pressure from business interests who have been quicker to spot commercial potential.

By the start of the 1960s several sports were in a poor state. Football had lost crowds all through the 1950s. Cricket was in a financial mess stemming from the steady decline in three-day county match receipts. Athletics was at the beginning of a decline in attendance that continued through to the 1960s. The popularity of Wimbledon was being undermined by the defection of many top stars to professional tennis. Only golf was relatively well off, benefiting from the adoption of the game by the upwardly mobile.

At the same time, thanks to television and the growth of international sport, top stars were better known than ever before. Opportunities to cash in on fame by grabbing lucrative fringe earnings were growing. In the 1950s a top footballer thought himself lucky to get the odd Brylcreem ad. Come the 1970s top footballers would need agents, tax consultants and offshore companies to handle their earnings.

The last 20 years have seen a second transformation of sport in this country, as dramatic as that between 1870 and 1900. The economy was at first relatively buoyant, the leisure market in particular was growing, expenditure on advertising and promotion was rising and the spread of television had brought sport to a much wider audience. The traditional forms of sport organisation faced crisis. Their power and authority was threatened by economic forces they seemed unable to come to terms with.

Individual entrepreneurs like Jack Kramer, Mark McCormack and, in the 1970s, Kerry Packer, picked upon the potential of the star system. Jack Kramer set up a professional travelling circus of tennis players in the 1950s. Top stars began to regard Wimbledon as a stepping-stone to a professional contract.

Mark McCormack saw the promotional value of a sporting image. He made Arnold Palmer a millionaire by lending his name to sport clothes and golf equipment. These fringe earnings rivalled the prize money Palmer made from playing the game. McCormack turned his three golf clients – Palmer, Nicklaus and Player – into global stars. He devised his own tournaments, set up matches staged especially for the television cameras and became the dominant figure in world golf. His organisation, International Management Group, comprises several companies including Trans World International, which produces pseudo sports programmes like *Superstars*. He employs hundreds of people in several countries, handling stars from various sports. Recently he has begun moving into athletics in anticipation of professionalisation.

Kerry Packer's involvement in cricket was a more pragmatic venture. He wanted the exclusive television rights for test cricket in Australia for his own television channel. When the cricket authorities refused, he set about signing up dozens of leading world cricketers and presented his alternative test series, in competition with the official one.

The cricket establishment was shocked to the roots. Cricketers in pink and blue flannels, white cricket balls, matches played under floodlights and on-pitch microphones were seen as an affront to tradition. After stormy battles – in and out of the courts – Packer got his television contract and wound up his cricket circus.

The economic forces represented by these brash entrepreneurs put the traditional sport authorities under considerable pressure. In particular the old hypocrisy of the amateur/professional division reached a crisis point. Cricket had abandoned the last vestiges of formal distinction between gentlemen and players in 1962. Tennis went open in 1967. Athletics has fought a rearguard action but it is now generally accepted that open athletics is the only way that the traditional authorities can retain control of the sport. There is already a lucrative professional road-running scene in the USA.

The economic basis of sport organisation was changing dramatically. Sports have six main sources of revenue: admission receipts, advertising, sponsorship, television fees, membership fees and fund-raising. (Football clubs can also make money from the trade in human beings called the transfer system.)

In the 1960s sponsorship began to grow as a source of finance. In the 1970s it rocketed to massive proportions. Sport sponsorship was not a totally new phenomenon. As early as 1908 Oxo had the marathon catering franchise for the London Olympics, and gave every runner an Oxo Athletes' Pack, with samples of their product. The *News of the World* had sponsored athletics events for some years.

But sponsorship money was not a major source of revenue for any sport. The first catalyst to growth came with the banning of cigarette advertising on television in 1965. Tobacco companies gradually realised that sport provided an alternative route to the screen. In 1966 less than £1 million went to sponsor sport events. By 1970 it was between three and five million pounds. The real boom then began. Sponsorship shot to £30 million by 1978.

The tobacco companies have recently been joined by the finance houses and insurance firms like Cornhill and Prudential. Cornhill's banners appeared 7,459 times on television in 1981 as a result of cricket sponsorship. Its awareness level (the number of people who mentioned Cornhill when asked to name all the insurance firms they could think of) jumped from 2 per cent in 1977 to 17 per cent in 1981.

Cricket, racing, motor sport, athletics and golf became major beneficiaries of the sponsorship boom. Football held out for a long time, hoping for a huge offer for its major competitions. Eventually in 1982 the League Cup became the Milk Cup. The new television sports like snooker and darts have attracted extensive sponsorship. Some tennis tournaments have benefited but Wimbledon continues to stand aloof. The All-England club, sustained by Wimbledon fortnight's mammoth income, is one of the few sport organisations that can afford to resist sponsorship.

Sponsorship money, then, has become a large and tempting carrot for sport to nibble at. But though there is a lot of sponsorship money available, there are also a lot of sports trying to get hold of it. Around ninety sports in this country battle for a share.

Obtaining television coverage is a crucial part of this battle. Some sponsorship money does go to non-televised events. Coca-Cola sponsor grassroots swimming, Pernod sponsor petanque in an attempt to launch both game and drink in Britain and show-jumping can lure sponsors with its up-market following. But for the most part the large sponsorship sums go to events that are televised.

This places television in a very powerful position. There are a few sports that are too popular for television to ignore – cricket, football, tennis, racing, golf and athletics, for example. These sports (with the exception of cricket) can hope that bidding between channels will make television fees worth having, even if not as high as they would like. As for the rest, television can pick and choose. There are maybe ninety sports that would love some television coverage. With only three real outlets, BBC, ITV and Channel Four, it is very much a buyer's market. If bowls authorities demand too high a fee, television will happily drop it and try table tennis instead.

So television gets much sport very cheaply. Sports are desperate to get coverage, not for the television fee, but because it opens up the possibility of sponsorship money. In order to get coverage a sport must offer something that will provide television entertainment. For many sports this has meant changes in rules, style and presentation. The growth of one-day cricket is just the tip of the iceberg.

The changing face of sport is due in equal part to the growth of television and the increased penetration of sport by capital. Sport has become an important aspect of advertising, promotion and marketing, and hence questions of image have become central. Few sports have remained untouched by these pressures.

Since the introduction of the Gillette Cup in 1963, the one-day match has become a central part of cricket. Many argue that the standard of cricket has been adversely affected by the one-day game but its popularity with the crowd, the sponsors and with television make it vital financially.

Athletics events are increasingly dominated by the pressure to present an array of stars and records. The public, reared on television, needs a Coe, an Ovett or an Alan Wells to lure it to the stadium. Once the spectators are there, promoters feel obliged to offer the sight of records tumbling, even if it means staging obscure and rarely run races such as the 4 × 800 metres relay featured at Crystal Palace in 1982.

The fickleness of sponsors has placed the sport in a state of perpetual uncertainty. The AAA centenary year was marred by the sudden withdrawal of the Championships sponsor, Nationwide, prompting a rush to find a replacement for the following year.

Television's particular focus on track events and in particular the short middle-distance races is changing the form of athletics meetings. Televised events now rarely feature a 10,000 metres and sometimes not even a 5,000 metres. One wonders how a future David Bedford or Brendan Foster can emerge with no races to run.

As in many sports, deals over brands of equipment are beginning to affect even the result of competitions. Poland banned their own crack high jumper Wzola from the 1982 European championships because he refused to wear the official brand of shoe. Britain's Steve Cram also had a row with officials during the championships when he refused to wear the official British shirt, which he found too hot.

Football has plunged on into deeper crisis pursuing the mythical family audience (a code word for middle-class consumers) with all-seated stadiums and executive boxes. The clothing firm Admiral changed the traditional football strips of many famous teams so that they could sell the new football strips in the latest colours to parents of boy footballers at inflated prices.

Leading football clubs continue to pressure the BBC to allow shirt advertisements. Liverpool get £50,000 per year for selling their shirt fronts. Being allowed to wear adverts on television would triple this sum.

Meanwhile Jimmy Hill continues to press for modifications to make the game more entertaining. The League decided not to outlaw the pass back to the goalkeeper, but have tried to clamp down on the professional foul. The main result is that during autumn 1982 so many were sent off that football looked like becoming a ten-a-side game.

Tennis has been transformed by the growth of the international circuit. With around ninety tournaments a year worldwide there is too much money chasing too few stars. In this sporting inflation the status of events becomes increasingly unclear. Is Lendl the true champ if Connors and McEnroe miss the tournament to play a lucrative, if leisurely, exhibition match elsewhere?

Even the top events are being transformed to suit television. In the US Championships many matches, including the men's final, have been played at night under floodlights. This is ideal for peak-time television, though the tennis may suffer somewhat. The 1979 Tournament of Champions Final in New York between McEnroe and Gerulaitis was played out in rain to fulfil a contract with NBC. Tennis, like athletics, has seen a decline in competition between nations. Top stars are often reluctant to play in the Davis Cup when there are richer pickings elsewhere.

Sport has become in the last 20 years both a part of the world of television spectacle and a branch of the advertising industry. The star system dominates sport. The danger is that the more attention, exposure and money that are concentrated at the very top of the pyramid, the more impoverished, drained and sterile the lower levels become.

When a mixed doubles between two couples (Chris Evert and John Lloyd v. Bjorn and Marianna Borg) staged in a tent in Battersea Park can be labelled the Love Match and sold to television all over the world for vast fees, the sports scene seems to have been reduced to absurdity.

Resistances and alternatives

The development of international competition, the growth of sport as television spectacle and penetration by advertising and promotion have not encountered much resistance. Nor have clear alternative directions emerged. But certain aspects of the dominant power and values of the sport system have been challenged. The organisation of labour in sport is often primitive and inadequate but from time to time has attempted to challenge the power of the authorities. The workers' sport movement between the wars began developing an alternative sport system. The rise of women's sport has confronted the dominance of male-centred values in the sport world.

Labour

Like any form of productive human activity sport depends ultimately upon the employment of human labour, although not necessarily waged labour. The main features of labour in sport have been an advanced division of labour with the maintenance of rigid hierarchies and extensive use of cheap, casual and voluntary workers.

Union organisation has in general been undeveloped, half-hearted, ineffectual or simply non-existent. The commercialisation of the last 20 years has given greater power to the top elite of star performers, without having much effect on others lower down.

Most sports have featured a highly developed division of labour from the early days. There are owners, bosses, workers of varying levels of skill, casual labour and voluntary unpaid labour. The power of ownership is important to most sports, whether based on the board of directors as in football, ownership of horses, stables and facilities as in racing, or control over access to stadiums as in boxing.

A lower level of labour carries out the owners' intentions by controlling the workforce. Managers in football, trainers in racing, committees and officials in many other sports control the nature of the performance.

The most prominent level of workers are the players. Their work is central to the sport as a commodity – it is their perform-ance that attracts the public and the television companies, their labour that makes the economic system of sport possible. Only in a few sports are the players employed as wage labour in the normal sense. Football and cricket are the main examples. In sports like tennis and golf players compete to win prize money. Boxers negotiate fees for particular fights. Athletes are officially amateur and unpaid, but top athletes can receive large sums in illicit pay-ments for appearances.

Most sports have a stratum of apprentices – people who are learning the trade. Like that of most apprentices their labour is particularly exploited. They are paid low wages and expected to do all sorts of menial tasks with no real relevance to the learning of skills. Apprentices in football are often expected to clean boots and dressing rooms and help out in ground repairs. There are no employment guarantees. Young footballers who fail to make the grade often find themselves on the street in their 20s with no qualifications and dismal job prospects.

Most sports also depend on layers of back-up work – ground maintenance, upkeep of pitches, courts or courses, administration and office staff. Occupations filled by those hoping to make it as performers – gym staff, handlers and sparring partners in boxing, stable lads in racing – are often particularly open to exploitation.

Much of this labour is casual. Sports stadiums depend on vast crews of doorkeepers, programme sellers and stewards, who cannot be employed on a regular basis. A great deal of labour in sport is voluntary. The amateur tradition and shortage of money in many sports caused a dependence upon voluntary work. But even more financially secure sports, like football and cricket, have often been able to rely on extensive assistance from supporters' clubs and members in providing stewards and help with cleaning and main-taining grounds.

Officials also work on a generally casual and often voluntary basis. Referees, umpires, ball boys and girls and line judges all perform crucial sport labour. Athletics has a particular depen-dence on voluntary officials.

The hierarchies in this world have often been maintained in a very rigid form. An old phrase in football holds that 'Directors direct, managers manage and players bloody well play.' Rows between players and authorities are common. The growth in the economic earning power of top players and the increased import-ance of sponsors and agents have only heightened these tensions, as the traditional authorities of sport find themselves undermined from both sides.

Union organisation in sport has never been strong. The volun-tary and amateur tradition and the high degree of casualisation, the organisation of sport in small units, the dominance of indi-vidualism and the degree to which players have to compete with each other to advance their careers do not encourage union orga-nisation.

As far as players themselves are concerned, it is not surprising that football, the most fully professional sport and the one with strongest working-class roots, should have the most developed union organisation in sport.

Professional footballers first formed a union in 1898 but had to struggle for ten years to gain recognition. In 1909 the union affiliated to the Federation of Trade Unions and the Football Associaton immediately withdrew recognition, threatening life suspension of its members. The union called a strike which even-tually collapsed despite some militant players going 14 weeks without pay, and it was forced to withdraw from the federation.

In 1912 the union lost another battle in the courts when it contested the high transfer fee being demanded for an Aston Villa player. Its contention that the fee was preventing the player from moving to another club was rejected by the judge, who awarded Villa costs. The lack of effective union power meant that, soon after the first world war, the Football League was able to reduce the maximum wage from £9 to £8 a week.

After the second world war, the Players' Union began to step up its campaign against the maximum wage and the retain and transfer system which gave clubs power to retain players against their will. A National Arbitration Tribunal in 1947 made some minor reforms and set up a joint standing committee with representatives of the Football League, Football Association and Players' Union. It recommended an increase in wage and bonus rates but once again rejected the union's main demands for abolition of the maximum wage and freedom of movement for players.

Internal struggles within the union led to changes at the top. Jimmy Hill took over the chair from Jimmy Guthrie. The union became the Professional Footballers' Association and entered its most successful phase. Pressure on the maximum wage grew, culminating in the threatened strike in 1960. After long negotiations the authorities conceded defeat and the maximum wage was abolished.

The battle over the retain and transfer system eventually reached the courts in the famous Eastham case. In 1960 the Newcastle United forward George Eastham asked to be put on the transfer list and his request was rejected by the club. He appealed to the Football League, which ruled that it was a matter between the player and the club.

Eastham refused to play for Newcastle and continued to fight, issuing a writ alleging that the club was depriving him of his right to earn a living at football. By the time the case reached the courts in 1963 Newcastle had backed down and Eastham had been transferred to Arsenal. Justice Wilberforce ruled that the rules of the Football League and the regulations of the Football Association concerning the retain and transfer system were an unreasonable restraint of trade. They were not actually illegal, but *ultra vires* – outside the law – and therefore were not legally binding.

This made some reform essential. The football authorities continued to resist complete freedom of contract and instead established an option system. This meant that the club had the option of renewing a contract but at the end of the second contractual period the player had the option of signing a new one or moving on at an agreed fee.

The Professional Footballers' Association has continued to press for greater contractual freedom but never with the militant commitment that swept away the maximum wage system. The increased international mobility of top players in the 1970s has placed the system under further strain. The old monopoly power of the English football authorities has been undermined by the lucrative financial opportunities for players in Europe and in the United States.

The first attempt at organisation in cricket was made by a group of Nottinghamshire professionals in 1881. They demanded a formal contract of employment and the right to organise their own matches. The county refused, dropped the cricketers involved and thereby lost that year's championship.

Cricketers never developed the same degree of organisation as footballers. This is partly because the game is less rooted in the working class, but more crucially because the workforce has an unusual composition – part amateur, part professional. This always left the professionals in a weak position.

The individual sports such as boxing, golf and racing have not developed organisations of a trade-union type. In amateur sports like athletics, there is no wage relation in any normal sense. There is no real contract or agreement over the labour of athletes. This has increasingly led to friction between the authorities and top athletes. As the authorities are not in any sense employers they have no real power to force athletes to compete. So they cannot guarantee to sponsors that stars will turn up.

In the last 20 years the top stars in a number of sports have become more powerful as their status has increased. But players' organisations are now more often like professional associations than trade unions. They are efficient at protecting the interests of the elite but usually lack the total commitment to solidarity needed to fight for better conditions at all levels of the hierarchy.

In tennis and golf, organisations of professional players have gained a significant degree of control over the game at the highest level. Women tennis players have found greater need for solidarity in their attempts to get a more equitable share of available prize money. Organisation in both these sports is dominated by top American stars.

In this country top cricketers secured a substantially better deal in the wake of the Packer affair when it was realised that the only way to ward off another Packer-style assault on test cricket was to increase players' earnings. But it was mainly the test players who benefited. The ordinary county cricketer does not earn much above the average industrial wage. (People in sport have a very short effective working life. Apart from snooker players, careers are generally over by the age of 40.)

Top athletes are organised together in the International Athletes' Club. Athletics is in a state of transition, with widespread undercover payments and open athletics just around the corner. The athletics meeting sponsored by Coca-Cola and organised by the IAC is generally the most star-studded and usually the most successful of the British season and this could be taken as an indication of the potential power of the top athletes. Certainly the traditional athletics authorities are in the midst of crisis.

The commercialisation of sport in the last 20 years has encouraged an individualised attitude to contracts. Top stars and their agents can negotiate huge earnings from a position of strength whilst people in the lower levels of sport are hard pressed to protect their basic interests. In particular the conditions of behind-the-scenes work essential to most sport remains generally poor and exploitative.

Workers' sport

One alternative to large-scale professionalised spectacle is suggested by the workers' sport movement. These organisations developed as deliberate alternatives to bourgeois dominance of sport and gained great popularity in the 1920s and 1930s, although they were less successful in Britain than on the continent.

Workers' sport had its beginnings and its greatest successes in Germany, growing initially out of the Social Democratic Party in the 1890s. It sought to provide alternative cultural experiences, based on proletarian values rather than bourgeois ones. By the beginning of the first world war there were 350,000 people in workers' sports organisations, but the real growth came in the 1920s.

By 1928 the workers' sport movements, still largely under SPD control, had two million members. Various organisations published a total of 60 newspapers read by eight hundred thousand people. In 1928 the communists split to form their own organisation, which had over one hundred thousand members by 1931.

Both organisations were smashed by the Nazis in the early 1930s. The movement generated a considerable degree of autonomous organisation. The German Workers' Cycling Association established a bicycle factory run on co-operative lines in the late 1920s.

Workers' sport also flourished in Belgium, Austria and Czechoslovakia. The Austrian Workers' Swimming Association gave one hundred thousand free swimming lessons in 1930. Membership of the Czechoslovakia labour sports movement reached over two hundred thousand. Similar organisations in Belgium, Denmark, France, Switzerland, Finland and Norway all had over twenty thousand members. In Britain the movement had less success. A National Workers' Sports Association formed in 1931 grew only slowly, although a series of workers' tennis tournaments was held at Reading Tennis Club in the 1930s. Workers' Wimbledon!

The movement had a strong commitment to internationalism. Many sporting visits were made and a series of Workers' Olympics was held as a counterpoint to the imperialist-dominated Olympics. The Czechs hosted a Workers' Olympics in Prague in 1921 and, whereas the official Olympics of 1920 excluded defeated countries Germany and Austria, the Prague games included them as a gesture of international working-class solidarity.

A Socialist Workers' Sports International was established and soon enrolled 1,300,000 members. By 1931 its membership topped two million, of whom 350,000 were women. The International organised the first official Workers' Olympics in 1925 in Germany, attended by 150,000 people. This was followed by a second event in Vienna in 1931 which involved 100,000 competitors from 26 countries.

A third Workers' Olympics was held in Antwerp in 1937, but the projected fourth games in Helsinki were cancelled after the outbreak of war. A People's Olympics scheduled for Barcelona in 1936 was cancelled after the opening parade when the fascist uprising began. But many athletes remained to fight in the battle for Barcelona and the ensuing civil war.

But the internationalism of the workers' sport movement was marked, as was politics more generally, by tensions between com-

munist and social democratic organisations. A separate organisation, the Red Sports International, set up in Moscow in 1921,
spent much of the 1920s locked in a power struggle with the
Socialist Workers' Sports International.

The RSI fought for an international sport organisation that,
under communist control, would be an active part of the class
struggle. The SWSI was more interested in creating a socialist
cultural organisation.

The RSI became involved in international sport festivals in
Moscow in 1928 and Berlin in 1931. It was not until after the rise of
the fascists in Europe that the two organisations began some
degree of co-operation. By then, of course, it was too late.

After the second world war this degree of internationalism could
not re-establish itself in the face of the cold war. But workers' sport
organisations in several countries provided an important base for
post-war developments. In Czechoslovakia the Proletarian Sports
Federation opened the way to the development of a socialist
physical culture.

After the war in West Germany the occupation powers effectively prevented the re-emergence of a politicised workers' sport
movement. The German Democratic Republic, on the other
hand, through the organisation Free German Youth, provided
lavish sport facilities to win political support. This policy, and the
emphasis on mass participation, had a great deal to do with the
startling success of the GDR in international sport in the
1970s.

Finland still has a workers' sport movement, separate from the
state sport organisations, with its own network of sport centres.
This separate history dates back to the expulsion of socialists from
the bourgeois sport organisations in the wake of political struggles
in 1917.

The expanded scale of sport in the post-war world and the
enormous cost of provision and organisation, together with the
general decline in international socialist links, has inhibited any
revival of autonomous workers' sports organisations.

Women in sport

The image of sport is heavily masculine. So even the participation
of women represents a challenge to the dominant values of the
sporting world. Increasingly the advances in women's sport, both
in numbers of participants and in standards of performance, are

challenging the notion that women's sport is a poor relation to the real thing.

Many factors have kept women out of sport. Parents teach basic physical skills like ball sense more effectively to boys than to girls. Education treats boys and girls differently. Girls are led to attach less importance to physical activity and facilities are often inadequate. The entry into adolescence introduces girls to notions of femininity that depend on physical passivity. The pressure on girls to help their mothers around the house restricts leisure time. This burden is frequently replaced by marriage and the greater burden of serving a husband and raising children. Sport facilities have often been designed without consideration of women as participants. Few women are active in sport organisation and so their voice is not heard nearly enough at policy level.

Despite all these factors, women's sport has seen major advances in the last 20 years. In 1960 women were still barred from marathons and the longest distance commonly run was 1500 metres. Today thousands of women regularly run long distances. Women's tennis and golf have become established professional sports. The myth of female frailty is firmly under assault. But it has still to be decisively dislodged.

Education has a complex place in the development of women's sport. The introduction of compulsory physical training in schools was an important break away from Victorian notions of female frailty and did expose girls to organised physical movement. But the separate traditions in male and female physical education have reinforced traditional views of gender difference.

It is not just that many sports are boys only. Even in mixed sex sports like athletics many events, such as pole vault, triple jump and even races from 400 metres and longer, are often barred to girls. Attitudes to sport in school are still heavily influenced by the notion that girls' bodies are less able. In fact there are no medical or physiological reasons why girls cannot take part in as wide a range of sports as boys of the same age.

But traditional notions of femininity are powerful. Many girls drop sporting activity early on in secondary school. Many women's sports developed in the context of taboos over physical contact between women. Netball, for example, involves less physical contact than basketball. In America a specially adapted form of half-court basketball was devised in the belief that women could not possibly be expected to do so much running.

These attitudes are further entrenched by the male dominance of sport organisation. The Sports Council has always been at least 90 per cent male. The current council of 23 has only two women, and of 18 principal officers only one is a woman. In the nine regions there is only one woman principal regional officer. Only 8 per cent of the other officials are women.

Facility provision is often dominated by the attitude that sport is for men. Pat Gregory of the Women's Football Association has been refused pitches by a local authority. Some authorities would appear to discriminate in favour of male teams at weekends in the belief that women can play during the week. Like most public facilities, the average sport centre has no proper provision for childcare.

Many of the myths about women and sport are now being exposed. There are no medical reasons to prevent women's participation during all phases of the menstrual cycle and there is some evidence that regular exercise and fitness may reduce period pains. Periods can cause fluctuations in performance but records have been set and medals won at all stages of the cycle.

In general there appear to be no medical reasons for reducing normal sporting activity in the earlier stages of pregnancy. Again, physical fitness tends to mean easier deliveries.

Since women have begun participating in sport in increasing numbers standards have improved dramatically. Women's world swimming records are rapidly catching up those of the men. The women's world 1500 metres record time would have won gold in the men's 1968 Olympic final. The women's world 400 metres record is within 18 seconds of the men's.

Norwegian Grethe Weitz has run the marathon in two hours twenty-five minutes, only fifteen minutes slower than the fastest men. Over one hundred women have now run the distance in less than two hours fifty minutes. It is now widely believed that women can perform better than men in ultra-long-distance events requiring stamina, because women's bodies are more efficient at burning fat reserves. Cross-channel swimming records are currently held by women, as is the all-comers' record for walking the 840 miles between John O'Groats and Land's End. Cyclist Beryl Burton, now in her 40s, still competes successfully with men in long-distance events.

In racing women were barred from all races except the Newmarket Town Plate until 1972. Since 1925 they have won that race 50 per cent of the time. In 1975 women jockeys were allowed in flat racing but it took the Sex Discrimination Act before they were allowed in steeplechasing the following year. Since then women have won 250 steeplechases.

But it is important to avoid the trap of comparing women's sport and men's sport, as if women's sport is important only when performances come close to men's. Women's sport should be seen in its own right. It all too seldom is. While there have been great changes in many sports, women are still treated as second-class citizens. Women golfers in Britain between the wars who wanted to turn professional found it impossible to get jobs. Nowadays the women's golf circuit in the United States consists of 40 tournaments with total prize money of around three million pounds.

But the sport still exists in the context of dominant sexist values. As a recent promotion stunt for women's golf a magazine featured photographs of top women golfers in the costumes and poses made famous by Hollywood stars like Jean Harlow and Marilyn Monroe.

Traditional values and attitudes still remain very powerful. Golf journalist Liz Kahn was thrown out of the men-only Royal and Ancient Clubhouse in 1978 while trying to report the Open Championship. At many golf clubs women are either excluded or given lower subscriptions with restricted access to the course and other limitations on membership.

Real open opportunity for women in sport will require many changes, a genuinely non-sexist educational system, an undermining of dominant attitudes about the inferior physical abilities of women, a greater responsibility taken by men for domestic labour, more social provision for childcare and more women in positions of influence in sport organisation.

The rising prominence of women's sport provides a base from which to attack the traditional masculine domination of sport. But the battle has still to be won.

Popular recreation

Recreation under capitalism is bound to be riddled by contradictions. Just as leisure itself is determined by the pattern of work, so forms of recreation are determined by the forms of social organisation that make them possible.

The ownership and control of open land, the development of the education system, the pattern of local authority provision, types of commercial provision and the publicity given to different activities all shape the forms of recreation available.

But people still make choices. They opt for some activities rather than others. They set up organisations to regulate and develop particular activities. They shape their own leisure, although always within limits.

Take skateboarding – a massive, if short-lived fad in the late 1970s. Skateboarding was made possible in part by technological development, providing more sophisticated wheels and flexible suspension. It was adopted by the street culture of early adolescence and the craze was fuelled by publicity. Huge numbers of boards were sold and a lucrative trade developed in protective helmets and pads.

Street accidents led to a demand for skate parks. Commercial interests and local authorities both responded. As provision improved the craze began to run out of steam. Manufacturers, stuck with over-capacity in little plastic wheel production, began promoting roller skates. A new craze, combining roller skating and listening to music on the new Walkman portable tape recorders, began.

Forms of recreation are not simply the outcome of freely exercised choice. But neither are they simply forced on people by a state intent on social control, or by entrepreneurs seeking profits. Recreation patterns are complex because all these factors are involved. This final section discusses some of these complexities.

Education

Most people first encounter organised physical activity at school. So the education system plays a formative role in shaping recreation habits.

The spread of universal education from the late nineteenth century heavily influenced the development of recreation in this country. There has never been one single dominant tradition in physical education but rather a number of strands.

Because the growth of state education took place alongside a continuing private sector, lower and upper classes were exposed to different traditions of physical education. As men and women physical education teachers received different forms of training, boys and girls were also exposed to different traditions.

The development of physical training in the board schools of the late nineteenth century stemmed in part from a desire to keep an eye on children during break times and to keep them away from bad company. It was partly a form of social control. But the early development of physical education was half-hearted. The 1870 Education Act allowed PT (physical training) for boys but did not prescribe it. An inspector's recommendation was needed before a school could adopt PT for girls.

A lot of early physical training was based upon military drill, despite considerable and growing opposition from many teachers. The state's concern to have fit workers was partly based upon the desire for a fit army, especially since the Boer War, when there had been considerable alarm about unfitness and malnutrition amongst troops. Much of the support for drill based PT came from military sources. Boys in the private and public schools played games that were supposed to train them for leadership, while the schools for the poor adopted forms of physical training and drill that would produce obedient and fit followers.

The opening of the Bergmann Osterberg College in 1885 heralded a different tradition in the physical education of girls and women. The founder, Mme Osterberg, wanted women to be taught by women and the men she initially engaged to teach cricket, tennis and vaulting were soon replaced by former students. A tradition of therapeutic gymnastics developed with an emphasis on health, grace and beauty.

Poor facilities were a big problem. In 1912 600 elementary schools had no playgrounds while a further 2,836 playgrounds were inadequate. The church schools had successfully opposed moves to enforce the improvement of facilities in the 1902 Education Act.

The state began to take recreation more seriously in 1906. The Education Act of that year talked of the importance of games in building physique and moulding character. It emphasised the potential improvements in health and *esprit de corps*. It said that the spirit of discipline, corporate life and fair play were acquired largely through sport.

So sport and recreation entered the education system as a fairly explicit tool for turning humans into subject citizens. But as so often, an expansionist aspiration eventually fell foul of a policy of contraction.

After the first world war a massive programme of government cuts inhibited the further development of physical education. Training courses for PE teachers were ended in 1923. There was to be no special training for men in physical education for ten years.

But games and sport were still often seen as useful for engineering consensus, papering over social division and preventing conflict. Prime Minister Stanley Baldwin said in 1926 that the greater the facilities for recreation, the better would be the health and happiness of the people and 'the closer will be the spirit of unity between all classes'.

The ruling-class delusion that sport is a magical panacea with the ability to erase class conflict is powerful. The massive unemployment, economic collapse and social deprivation of the 1920s and 1930s gave rise to a renewed interest among establishment figures in leisure provision.

In 1925 a National Playing Fields Association was formed under the presidency of the Duke of York. Successful financial appeals led to the establishment of 800 playing fields over the next few years.

Concern over fitness brought closer connections between the physical education and medical professions. A British Medical Association report of 1936 said that 40 per cent of people between 14 and 40 needed, but did not get, regular physical recreation.

With fear of war growing, a National Fitness Campaign was launched, without conspicuous impact. There was a renewed attempt to use recreation as a disguised form of military training. In a 1937 debate Aneurin Bevan denounced the need to evoke national well-being to fund recreation, saying that individual well-being was a sufficient justification.

The second world war left its mark on physical education. The use of assault courses in military training spread downwards into the schools. Primary schools developed 'jungle gymnasia' and secondary schools took up circuit training.

After the war there was a gradual expansion in provision. A number of tensions between different traditions continued in importance. The battle between training and recreation, between proponents of military-style drill and advocates of games for recreation and enjoyment, continued.

An increased interest in dance and movement in girls' physical education teaching sharpened the debate between those who saw physical education as tied primarily to competitive sport and those who emphasised individual body movements.

The development of the outward-bound schools and the Duke of Edinburgh award schemes in the 1950s represented a return to a more aristocratic tradition of individualism. These schemes were supposed to foster courage, initiative, self-reliance and leadership. This note of macho rugged individualism was in some degree opposed to the already well-established emphasis on team games.

In the 1960s and 1970s a new set of tensions in the syllabus developed between the adherents of the traditional sports – football, rugby and cricket for boys, hockey and netball for girls – and the introduction of newer and more novel ones. The improved level of educational provision brought basketball, volleyball, trampolining, tennis and many other sports into more common use. The growth of multi-cultural education brings new problems for physical education teachers, who are going to have to respond to demands that traditional Asian games be provided for and also come to terms with the Muslim and Hindu attitudes of disapproval towards physical activity for girls.

Underlying many of these tensions are two conflicting attitudes about physical education: one that it has some benefit for society as a whole, the other that its benefits are primarily individual. But perhaps the most tangible effect of organised games at school has been to put many people off sport for the rest of their lives.

Leisure between the wars

The inter-war years saw the growth of many existing participation sports and the development of new ones. Fitness-centred activities like hiking and cycling grew enormously in popularity. They attracted larger lower-middle and working-class involvement and generated a range of autonomous organisations.

The spread of municipal provision extended the popularity of swimming, tennis and bowls. New commercially run ice rinks became popular. Cycling had enjoyed continued popularity since the late nineteenth century and the development of the safety cycle and the pneumatic tyre. The group cycling trip was well established.

There was a new level of interest in physical activity and fitness, and a whole range of organisations – YMCA, YWCA, Boys'

Brigade, Scouts and Guides – had expanded their physical recreation programme. The influence of religious, military and imperialist ideas in these organisations is well known. It is much harder to know how much these ideas appealed to members. Many may well have joined to use the organisations' facilities without subscribing to the ideas they peddled.

Hiking, rambling and camping grew enormously in popularity. The Youth Hostel Association was formed in 1930. By the following year it had 73 hostels and 6,000 members. It grew throughout the 1930s and by 1939 had 279 hostels and 83,417 members. The new London Country Council Evening Institutes introduced classes in physical exercise, gymnastics and swimming.

The Keep Fit Movement, launched by women in the north-east, had 127 women turn up for its first class in 1929. By the following year it was running nine classes for about five hundred people a week. The Women's League of Health and Beauty was launched in 1929. By 1933 it had 30,000 members and an incredible 120,000 by 1937. It appears to have developed a distinct political inflection. During an Albert Hall performance in 1933 it staged a mime symbolising the reconciliation of capital and labour (an interesting contrast to the workers' sport movements thriving on the continent at this time).

During this period, much leisure activity seems to have centred around the lower middle and working class, outside the traditional structures of organised sport. There appears to have been a widespread interest in active physical leisure, but generally in a noncompetitive form. People often set up their own organisations and activities, separate from both state and commercial outlets. But cultural-political organisations like the workers' sport movements do not not seem to have attracted much support in Britain. Mental and physical activities are more compartmentalised in this country. So coherent interaction of activity and ideas is limited. Sport and politics are seen as very different aspects of social life.

Fun in the 1970s

The relative affluence of the post-war era transformed leisure activity. The spread of television and car ownership, and the growth of the record industry in the 1950s and 1960s, encouraged more passive forms of leisure. The great outdoors no longer beckoned as it had in the 1930s. The new focus of leisure time was the family home. The acquisition of material goodies – fridges, hi-fis and the like – was an important part of home buildings. The do-it-yourself industry grew to service the new passion for home improvement.

But these developments have in the 1970s reversed. A new enthusiasm for physical leisure has arisen. People have become more concerned with fitness and health. The well-documented link between smoking and heart and lung disease has finally begun to make some inroads into smoking habits. (The tobacco companies still market their more lethal blends in the third world with undiminished zeal.) Hostility to processed foods, particularly bread, has had a growing impact on eating habits. Nonetheless, over-consumption and unhealthy products are still major killers.

This new enthusiasm for fitness and exercise has a contradictory character. The passion for exercise is largely confined to the middle class and has spawned a thriving health and fitness industry. Track suits are now high fashion, a form of sport chic.

But the fitness boom also breeds criticism of passive consumption. Getting more exercise, eating sensibly and leading a more active life lead people to see more clearly the harmful aspects of the food, drink and media industries and of passive forms of leisure.

The new interest in fitness has shown itself most obviously in the huge growth of running. The development of the jogging craze in America was treated largely as a joke. It certainly had its comic aspects. People jogging alongside highways sometimes passed out from the fumes. When jogging crossed the Atlantic much of the early advice passed between runners was concerned with how to deal with the smirks, sniggers and cat-calls of non-runners.

The immense success of mass fun-runs and gigantic people's marathons have gradually shown that the enthusiasm for running is more than a craze. Last year in Britain 100,000 people ran in marathons up and down the country. Many times that number probably run regularly for exercise or fun.

The new fun-running undermines many of the dominant values of sport. The marathon used to be represented as the ultimate challenge, the Everest of athletics. Only highly-trained men were capable of completing the course. Women were not even allowed to run the distance. This mystique has been shattered. The distance has now been run by thousands of ordinary people after a year or so of part-time training. It has been run by men and women of all ages. A 78-year-old man finished in the 1981 London marathon. It has been run by people recovering from heart attacks, diabetes and cancer.

Women have had great success. Joyce Smith, who is 44, has been an athlete most of her life but took up the marathon only three years ago. She finished the last London marathon in two-and-a-half hours, within twenty minutes of the fastest man. Her performances have inspired many other women to take up running. Fourteen hundred women ran in the 1982 London marathon. Few things have so effectively undermined the myth of female frailty.

Large-scale popular running is also not very competitive. Everyone runs to his or her own standards and if people compete it is largely against their own limitations. Runners give each other a lot of mutual support.

The people's marathons have broken down the sharp divisions between spectators and participants too. Because the runners are so obviously ordinary people rather than highly-trained full-time athletes, many spectators realise that they too could run. Many who watched in 1981 ran in 1982. Runners often refer to the immense support and encouragement they get from the crowd.

The giant marathons are certainly a form of spectacle, but not of the normal star-laden variety where all focus is on the winners. Television commentators soon found out that the people's marathons cannot be treated simply as a race.

Taking the spotlight off stars breaks down the normal distinction between the elite and the grassroots. Usually we are encouraged to see top athletes as a different breed of humankind. It is hard to go on believing that if you have run the same course in the same race, even if it did take you an hour longer.

Running can be a spontaneous, simple and unstructured activity. It can be done anywhere, singly or in groups. It needs no elaborate equipment. There is no need to be subject to the rule of a coach, manager or boss figure. It is a highly effective way of keeping the weight down, the muscles in trim and generally staying fit. Many people also find that it feels good to do and feels good afterwards.

The benefits are not all physical. Regular runners talk of feeling more alert, being more able to relax, sleeping better and feeling more self-confident.

Of course there are negative aspects to the whole running phenomenon too. The macho-competitive element is still present. The concept of running a marathon has become rather over-dramatised. You aren't a real runner until you've done it.

The very popularity of marathon running has had undesirable effects, such as the premature involvement of child runners. Eleven-year-old Cheryl Page was banned by the AAA from running in the London marathon. Many doctors believe that excessive forms of exercise by growing children can cause bone damage and malformation. There is concern that the marathon boom could trigger a wave of child runners, pushing their bodies too hard.

The marathon business has become very commercialised too. Trade names emblazon everything that moves. Public relations firms jostle to get their clients on the screen. Application forms for the London marathon are accompanied by an enclosed leaflet advertising New Balance Shoes, a firm owned by two of the marathon organisers. People are now so anxious to get into the limited entry marathon that the procedure is surrounded by queues for the post, threats of lawsuits, allegations of bribery and the likely development of an illicit market in entry permits.

A whole new sector of the sport clothing market has opened up. Once it was possible to have a pair of plimsolls, a white vest and shorts and a tube of vaseline and be a world-class runner. Now, if you believe the adverts, no Sunday jogger is complete without a pacemaker digital watch, a runner's radio, a waist pouch, a security wrist band for keys, weighted training gloves, special reflective bands for night running and a personalised computer training program.

Training shoes and track suits sell for anything up to £90 each. And, if you're really serious, a special aerobic exerciser, consisting of a face mask and a couple of back cylinders, will simulate the beneficial effects of altitude training. It will also set you back around £100.

The conditions in which popular recreation takes place are established by the nature of the economic system and the network of social institutions built upon it. In a capitalist society any popular leisure activity is also going to be highly commercialised. Change within sport alone cannot have dramatic results. But, if a more humane, more egalitarian and less oppressive form of sport is worth fighting for, then it is important to examine the existing organisation of sport and possible alternatives.

The next chapter looks at state policy towards sport and the existing patterns of provision. The final one suggests the issues that socialists need to consider if they are to argue for alternatives.

5.

Sport and the State

In many countries the state has developed a systematic policy towards sport and put it into practice. Cuba is an excellent example. This has not happened in Britain. The recurrent pattern has been one of *ad hoc* improvisations, carried out by a variety of separate, largely voluntary organisations, with unco-ordinated plans and persistent financial problems. This chapter will examine the Sports Council and the problems of a state policy towards sport.

I have outlined the development of sport in England in terms of shifting patterns of dominance. The artistocratic patronage of the eighteenth century was replaced in importance by the rise of sport institutions dominated by sections of the upper-middle class of the late nineteenth century. These predominantly amateur-paternal sport organisations dominated English sport until the post-war era. From the early 1950s the growing internationalisation of sport, its penetration by capitalist commerce, the effect of television and the associated growth of sponsorship gave birth to a new form of patronage – the economic patronage of sponsorship. Only in the last 20 years has the state played much of a role.

The state intervenes in the field of sport and leisure in three main ways. First, it tries to ban certain activities . I have already mentioned attempts to outlaw bowls and football in the sixteenth and seventeenth centuries. There was the wave of anti-cruel-sport legislation in the nineteenth century. Bare-knuckle boxing remains illegal and a new lobby is under way to ban boxing altogether.

Second, the state regulates and licenses activities. The most notable example is the control of betting and gaming. The whole social practice of gambling, and hence horse-racing and

greyhound-racing in their current forms, is in no small part determined by state legislation. The 1960 Betting and Gaming Act
brought the off-course betting shop into being. In 1953 there had
been 4,000 arrests for street betting in London, but by 1967 there
were a mere three. A vastly profitable and legal industry had been
created.

Third, the state provides facilities. The long fight by the labour
movement gradually forced the reductions in working hours and
increase in public holidays that made leisure time a possibility for
urban workers. Conservative concern with social control and liberal pressure for social reform led to a growth in municipal provision
of parks, wash-houses and swimming pools. But the scale should
not be exaggerated. In 1909 there were more public hard courts for
tennis in Hamburg than in the whole of England.

The rise of the Sports Council

State involvement in leisure was largely *ad hoc* and local from the
mid-nineteenth century until the 1930s. The first impetus towards a
central coherent organisation grew out of concern over national
fitness. The international capitalist crisis of the 1930s had caused
severe cuts in public spending and unemployment for between two
and three million people. Children left school at 14 but could
obtain unemployment benefit after 16 only by attending the compulsory Junior Instruction Centres.

The rise of fascism in Europe prompted British establishment
figures to compare the nationalistic fervour of fascist youth movements with the supposed listless, apathetic state of Britain's youth.
Within the ruling classes, both those who admired and those who
feared the rise of fascism felt some need for action. These half-
formed feelings combined with the growth of a consciousness
about physical culture stemming from the medical and physical
education professions. The many existing voluntary bodies also felt
the need for a forum to co-ordinate activities.

The Central Council for Recreation and Training (as it was then
called) was formed in 1935, through the initiative of Phyllis Col-
son, a physical education organiser. It had royal patronage and the
support of the Board of Education. It brought together organisations of sport and physical education, along with a large medical
presence. The declared aim was 'to help improve the physical and

mental health of the community through physical recreation by developing existing facilities for recreative physical activities of all kinds and also by making provision for the thousands not yet associated with any organisation'.

The government was also prompted to act by concern with fitness. It formed a National Fitness Council, which had a brief and unhappy life. The outbreak of war eventually defused the paranoia over national fitness. After the war the CCPR was to turn its attention to the provision of facilities and, in particular, to the development of National Recreation Centres.

The CCPR was an independent body, but most of its income came from statutory grants. So in the late 1940s and 1950s it featured in post-war reconstruction, along with the growth of the welfare state and the expansion of state intervention in the mixed economy.

Its most significant achievement at this time was the establishment of seven National Recreation Centres. These provided residential facilities for a variety of sports. The centres mainly served more committed sports people and part of their role was to raise standards at the highest levels to boost British chances in international competition.

The physical education world was becoming increasingly concerned with preparing for international competition. English assumptions of sporting dominance were shaken when Hungary's footballers beat England 6–3 at Wembley in 1953. English sporting administrators felt threatened by the growing power of both America and the communist countries in international sport. There was a reaction against the traditional amateur-paternal ethos.

The CCPR set up the Wolfenden Committee in 1957 to recommend ways in which statutory bodies could help promote the general welfare of the community in sport and leisure. Confusion between developing an elite and serving the general interest is a typical feature of English debates over sport policy.

The Wolfenden report, *Sport and the Community* (1960), found that there was an overwhelming case for statutory financing of sport. It expressed concern that sport, which then came under the Minister for Education, was a low priority. The report recommended the establishment of a sports council of six to ten people to control expenditure of around £5 million per year.

A distinct political consensus was developing. In the 1959 election campaign both major parties were against a minister for sport but in favour of a sports council along the lines of the Arts Council. But the victorious Conservatives then did little. Lord Hailsham, given special responsibility for sport, increased government expenditure, but dragged his feet over the proposed sports council.

Labour came to power in 1964 committed to a sports council but, as a statutory body required legislation, they initially set up an advisory council. Seven years of uncomfortable negotiation followed as the relationship between this advisory council and the CCPR was worked out. The problems were a reflection of a typical desire on the part of the British state to prevent institutions appearing to be state controlled. A Minister for Sport would be answerable to parliament, whereas a quasi-independent council, even if appointed by the government, would be outside the parliamentary political process.

By 1968 a compromise had been arrived at. In 1969 Denis Howell, the Minister with responsibility for sport, was moved from the Department of Education and Science to the Ministry of Housing and Local Government. Sport funding was no longer a part of the education budget. It acquired greater status as a result.

The 1970 Conservative government resolved to establish a statutory and executive sports council which would disburse funding. This would effectively take over many of the functions of the CCPR, which was offered the option of self-destruction. There was strong feeling in the CCPR against this and in the event the Sports Council took over the full-time staff and resources of the CCPR, which then re-structured itself into an independent forum of sport organisations.

The character of the two organisations has been very different. The Board of the Sports Council is appointed by the Minister and so is a quasi-autonomous part of the state. The CCPR is somewhat more democratic, being composed of representatives of the various governing bodies of sport.

The Sports Council and sport in the 1970s

The new executive Sports Council was established in 1971 by Royal Charter. Its brief again reflected the conflict between the needs of the elite and the grassroots. It was supposed to develop knowledge of sport and physical recreation in the interests of social welfare and to encourage the attainment of high standards in conjunction with the relevant governing bodies.

The prevailing wisdom in the early 1970s was that leisure time would increase, participation would rise and that there was serious under-provision for sport and recreation. Given a legacy of chronic under-provision, and an uphill struggle for adequate funding, the most significant advance has been the expansion of sport centres. In 1964 there was just one purpose-built sport centre in the whole of England and Wales. By 1972 there were still only 30. By 1978 there were 350.

The prediction of rising rates of participation has proved to be true. So, in a sense, with over three million people on the dole, has that of increased leisure time. As funding has become progressively tighter, the emphasis has switched from the provision of new facilities to the maximum exploitation of existing ones. In recent years the Sports Council has begun to identify low-participation groups – the disabled, the over-50s, and women, especially those with young children. The final chapter questions the ability of the Council to deal with the problems it identifies.

Since the mid-1970s, the inner cities have increasingly been seen as areas of special concern. The drive to develop sport facilities in these areas stems partly from a progressive liberal reformism. But it is also clear that many policy makers see inner-city sport as a way of defusing social tension, as a form of social control. Since the riots of 1981 it has suddenly become much easier to obtain funding for inner-city projects. Nothing loosens the purse strings like panic.

State policy and social reality

No political party in Britain has a clear policy for sport. The Liberals have just produced an extensive document on the arts but nothing equivalent on sport. Conservative Central Office told me that 'we don't generate policy when we're in office'. The Labour Party support the right of access to common land, oppose apartheid in South African sport and oppose the sale of sports grounds into private hands. The SDP are still working on it. Other parties of the left and right have little to say on the subject.

So policy is formed by a combination of Sports Council action, ministerial whim and – crucially – local authority policy and spending patterns. Up until around 1976 the expansion proposed by the Sports Council was in relative harmony with the aims (as opposed to the actual practice) of government policy. But commitment to expanded provision has come under increasing pressure. Restrictions on state spending threaten public provision. At the same time the rise of sponsorship is re-shaping sport in ways that bypass the Sports Council. Privatisation increasingly threatens public sport facilities. The Sports Council's response is totally inadequate.

Its current strategy advocates a budget rising from the current £22 million to £46 million in 1987. Realising that this prospect is fairly remote, it outlines the effects of limited growth and standstill budgets over the same period. Yet the strategy fails to highlight the crisis in public provision, does nothing to pinpoint the causes and is of no help in fighting cutbacks. At a time when the gulf between rich and poor in sport is widening, the Sports Council not only has no effective strategy but fails to recognise that there is a problem.

Public spending cuts affect sport provision in many ways. Few new facilities are planned. Old ones are threatened with closure. Staff cuts reduce opening hours. Lower spending on maintenance leads to collapse of facilities. Poorly maintained tennis courts drive people away, reducing revenue and encouraging further staff cuts. In some places cuts in ground staff have encouraged vandalism. Mobile security services have then been called in – a depressing manifestation of the growth of a law and order society. Higher fees reduce use. In Wandsworth swimming pool and weekday tennis fees have doubled in the last year. The CCPR estimated that in 1980 £20 million was lost in spending on sport and recreation. In the same year the Thatcher government offered a £50 million bribe to move the Olympics from Moscow.

In sport, as in the health service, an impoverished public sector sits side by side with a booming, and expensive, private sector. Major spectator sports already cast their eyes mainly at the affluent end of the market. Football has thrown resources into the provision of elaborate executive boxes. For £120 Keith Prowse offered a top-price seat at Wembley. The price included a champagne reception and a four-course meal. But the highlight was a buffet party with Jimmy Tarbuck afterwards. For an outlay of £6,000 Abbey Executive Services will provide 20 Wimbledon Final

Day tickets, along with a luxury lunch, limitless wine and strawber-
ries and cream. But it is not just spectator sports that are being
transformed. Private clubs thrive on the boom in physical leisure.
At the Cannon Sports Centre in the City of London city execu-
tives' subscriptions of £350 per year are often paid by their bosses,
who can claim part of the cost against corporation tax.

Of course a large proportion of sport and recreation provision
has always been in private hands. Our two major spectator sports,
football and cricket, have always jealously guarded their facilities
against encroachment by the public. The premier tennis facilities
are maintained for the year-round benefit of a tiny elite, on the
huge profits of Wimbledon fortnight. In the mid-1950s, when only
47 of Britain's 130 athletic tracks were in public hands, Finland had
500, and Sweden 800 for a population of 7 million. At a time when
open land is being gobbled up by property developers, school
recreation grounds, seen as surplus to requirements, are also being
sold for development.

Privatisation poses a greater threat to public provision. Local
authorities are increasingly prepared to offload their traditional
responsibilities for short-term gain. Privatisation is a new form of
asset-stripping in which assets belonging to us all are sold to private
capitalists at knock-down prices. The much touted increase in
efficiency that privatisation is supposed to bring is largely a myth,
as those unfortunate enough to live under the Wandsworth Tories
are currently discovering.

Privatisation results in either a worse or a more expensive
service, or in greater exploitation of workers. Often it means all
three. Any hope of public accountability is also lost.

Already some boroughs, such as Hillingdon in London, are
experimenting with a form of halfway house on the road to privatisation, whimsically referred to as an entrepreneurial partnership.
The Manor Leisure Centre near Peterborough, complete with
sports hall, cricket and football pitches, swimming pool and tennis
courts, has been put up for sale. After closing tennis courts in
Carshalton Park at weekends to save overtime, the London
borough of Sutton then made three out of five available for
exclusive private use. Richmond Park golf course currently breaks
even and thus pays for itself, providing a high popular public
service. But the government are determined to privatise it.

Private enterprise has its eyes on the potential profits in this field. Commercial Union, Dunlop, Debenhams, MacAlpine and Watneys have formed a consortium, Cavendish Leisure, to promote the privatisation of swimming pools. Their strategy is to blame restrictive practices by NALGO and their claim that admissions at pools cover only 18 per cent of the costs suggests that they would charge a lot more.

They will probably get ministerial support. A campaign last year to get public swimming baths to open early in the morning failed to gain Minister of Sport Neil MacFarlane's backing. MacFarlane does, however, appreciate the value of early-morning swimming. He swims 20 lengths every morning – in a private pool.

Unfortunately the Sports Council shows little awareness that these developments constitute a problem. Its current strategy seems to involve active encouragement of entrepreneurial partnerships.

The Sports Council has consistently failed to give any encouragement to progressive forces. On the two most public aspects of sports policy, apartheid and tobacco sponsorship, the Council has tried desperately to avoid taking a clear position. On apartheid, the report of its recent fact-finding tour does little to convince readers that the Council is in the forefront of the battle to maintain the spirit of the Gleneagles agreement. On tobacco, it is reluctant to take a stand against such a major source of money. Its discussions have no doubt been aided by the presence on the Council up till 1982 of Sir James Wilson, chairperson of the Tobacco Advisory Council.

The Sports Council is a profoundly undemocratic body. It is run by a board appointed by the Minister and accountable only to him. It is also heavily male-dominated and until very recently has done little to acknowledge, let alone alleviate, the factors inhibiting women's involvement in sport. Its recent prestigious international conference, Sport and People, had not a single woman speaker, apart from the closing address by the organiser. It has lost touch with the grassroots of sport. It has evolved a strategy incompatible with the current economic situation and has failed to acknowledge fully the threat to past achievements.

6.

Arguments for Socialism

This chapter offers some suggestions for transforming the structure, organisation and values of sport. It draws on the socialist critique of sport discussed in Chapter Two. But it rejects the view that the whole institution of sport is simply incompatible with socialism. Instead it argues that competitive sport is a more complex, varied and adaptable activity than its critics suggest.

The first section argues the need for a genuinely egalitarian sport system, with adequate facilities and finance. A case is made for social ownership and democratic control. The second section examines areas where discussion is needed to clarify the way ahead. The place of elite sport, and of national sport and the nature of competition in sport, should be debated more openly. Dominant ideas and values do not change overnight. Nor can they be legislated away. Support for socialist principles must be won. The third section discusses the problems facing those arguing for a socialist transformation of sport. We need a strategy for making socialist ideas popular.

Sport for all

The first aim of any socialist strategy ought to be the achievement of an egalitarian sport system with adequate facilities available to all. The Sports Council's own slogan, 'Sport For All', provides a fine starting point. It expresses an egalitarian intention, but one that can be realised only through socialism. Only with social ownership of resources under democratic control could we have genuine sport for all. Socialists should seize on the contradictions lying behind this slogan and press those within sport to see its implications. The rhetoric of the policies behind Sport For All expresses admirable principles. But good intentions must founder if they fail to confront social reality.

We live in a society with massive inequalities of wealth and income. A small proportion of the population owns and controls a vast proportion of the country's land, property and production. Giant commercial enterprises have great power to define the whole field of leisure. So the achievement of Sport For All depends on broader social changes.

But it is still important to spell out the preconditions for achieving Sport For All. First, we need to define what is meant by the phrase. Then we need to develop a strategy for the provision and financing of adequate facilities. This book will argue that this requires an extension of social ownership. Finally, we need to build in democratic control at all levels.

I take Sport For All to mean that the means of sporting activity should be available to everyone in the forms and at the times that people can best use them. It does not mean that everyone *has* to be involved in sport. People have a right to take other forms of physical exercise or shun exercise altogether, however irresponsible this may be!

Taking Sport For All seriously involves confronting sexism and racism. Positive discrimination is needed to undo a long history of white male dominance. Dominant stereotypes of sporting activity must be combated. Posters advertising sport halls frequently feature boys but not girls and white but not black or Asian children.

But the fight for genuine opportunity for all involves more than being non-racist and non-sexist. It means actively confronting the legacy of past practices that have perpetuated racism and sexism. Positive discrimination is needed to involve more women and black Britons in the running of sport. There is a need for far more women and black sport teachers and motivators. Action must be taken to ensure that schools and sport centres always have as good facilities for girls and women as they do for boys and men. The need for change here is closely linked to broader struggles. The fight for creches in sport centres is part of a broader struggle for full social provision for the needs of pre-school children.

The degree to which these problems are recognised within sport administration varies greatly. The regional strategy of the Greater London and South East Council for Sport and Recreation has worthy intentions, although its ability to promote them effectively in the present economic climate is doubtful. By contrast, the regional strategy of the West Midlands mentions the problems of mothers with young children but has virtually nothing to say about women on the whole.

Change in sport, and attitudes to it, depend in part on education. The practices of physical education are outside the scope of this book. But education could play a major role in undermining the notion that sport is for the boys. To date education has tended to reinforce gender roles and attitudes to sport. Attitudes to race are rather different. Black children who show an ability for sport are often encouraged at the expense of pressure to maintain their academic studies. The underlying stereotype is that black people are only good at sport, not academic work. The notion of sport as a way out of the ghetto has brought material success for an elite few, but is a dangerous cul-de-sac for thousands more.

The struggle to change attitudes will mean little without adequate facilities. Despite the work of the Sports Council in the 1970s, we are still very short of local multi-purpose sports halls. Britain has only one indoor athletics track. France has twelve and West Germany five. Our 64 indoor tennis courts compare unfavourably with the 1,200 in France. Since the second world war Holland, France and West Germany have each spent three times as much per head on sports provision as Britain.

Yet there is great social value to be obtained from money spent on sport. A fit healthy population is a great social asset, and spending on sport has hidden benefits for public spending as a whole. The radical solution to the problem of the high cost of health service provision has always been to place much greater emphasis on prevention. Discouraging alcohol and tobacco abuse, and encouraging healthy eating habits and regular exercise could eventually transform the pattern of health care. Cuba places great emphasis on the benefits of physical activity. Babies are introduced to exercise through play almost from birth.

Sport funding could be improved in a number of ways. Thousands of millions are spent each year on gambling. A small portion is taken in tax, but none of it is earmarked specifically for sport.

In 1981 betting duty on the football pools netted £184 million. A mere 12 per cent of this would be almost enough to double the

Sports Council's grant. But there is no sound reason why the hugely profitable betting industry should remain in private hands at all. Many countries operate state lotteries. If we are to have gambling (and many argue that like tobacco and alcohol it cannot be legislated out of existence) then let us at least use the profits constructively.

At present, certain areas of sport get substantial funds through tobacco sponsorship. The great irony is that a physical activity like sport should be supported by such a physically destructive product. The argument in favour of tobacco sponsorship has always been that some sports depend on it. This argument is somewhat spurious. Even cricket is now getting as much help from the finance houses and insurance firms as it is from tobacco. If money has to go from tobacco to sport let it be through a levy on tobacco company profits.

This principle – that those who threaten health and fitness should pay for its promotion – is perfectly viable, even in the heart of capitalism. Long Beach in California levies a tax on local oil-drilling companies to pay for sport and recreation facilities in the area.

One broader strategy option is to take into public ownership not just unprofitable sectors but precisely those profitable ones which could help support other areas. It is bizarre to have an impoverished sports system amidst industries growing rich by selling rackets, clubs, bats, track suits, jogging shoes, swimwear and other sporting paraphernalia.

But the problem of facilities is not simply one of finance. It is also one of social organisation. The economic climate has forced the Sports Council to switch emphasis from the provision of new facilities to the more efficient use of existing ones. School facilities, for example, should be made available for community use at evenings, weekends and during school holidays. Unfortunately this still happens fully only in a minority of cases. For too many years it has been all talk and no action. The crisis now facing education authorities from cutbacks in state spending and falling rolls ought to force fresh thinking. School facilities *are* community facilities. The fall in pupil numbers provides a perfect opportunity to bring school and community closer together.

The enormous amount of recreation land in private hands presents a greater problem. The utilisation of private playing fields is appallingly low. There is no social justification for fields standing empty day after day, week after week. Open land is rapidly becoming more scarce and should be controlled for the social good.

Facilities alone are no good. They are there to be used. There is a great shortage of teachers and motivators – people able to encourage physical activity. Sport authorities in this country have only recently begun to appreciate the value of motivators. Countries that have put more resources into supporting this role have generally seen a significant increase in participation rates.

Much of this work can be on an informal basis. In China, factory workers can attend coaching clinics and workshops in exchange for coaching their workmates when they return. This is a valuable social principle, based on sharing knowledge rather than treating it as private property.

Social ownership of facilities would have other advantages. Take the case of football, for almost a century the most popular spectator sport in the country. At the highest level, the Football League clubs are structured like capitalist enterprises, but controlled mainly by businessmen for influence or as a hobby, rather than for profit. Their product, football, has a large working-class audience, with no power over the sport often regarded as 'theirs'.

Football is currently in financial crisis, with clubs as famous as Wolverhampton Wanderers coming close to bankruptcy. The causes are complex and those in and around the game endlessly debate the respective importance of high wages, spiralling transfer fees, hooliganism, quality of football, professional fouls, too much television coverage and the changing face of society. Underlying it all is a pattern of financial mismanagement with roots in the late 1960s and early 1970s.

A moral panic over hooliganism led many in the game to think in terms of appealing to a more affluent consumer. They saw the way ahead in terms of all-seated stadiums, executive boxes complete with colour TV and cocktail cabinet and the mythical 'family audience'. Grandiose plans were put into motion up and down the country for expensive new stands. Meanwhile gates continued to fall steadily through the 1970s.

While gates declined, expenditure rocketed. Millions were borrowed to erect new stands. Transfer fees spiralled towards the million pounds per player level and competitive bidding drove wages up rapidly. Clubs borrowed heavily and landed themselves with huge interest payments at a time of falling revenue. Rising interest rates made things worse. Football clubs have few tangible assets. Players' values are too erratic for financiers to rely on. Grounds and stadiums may be worth a lot but their value can be realised only by ceasing to play. Football could become an asset-strippers' playground – particularly where grounds are in urban areas suitable for property development.

Football can still attract around 20 million people a year and television fees of £2,500,000 for a year's league matches alone. But it is unable to sort out its own financial problems. The passionate desire for success leads directors towards self-destruction. The financial collapse of Chelsea in the mid-1970s, brought about by huge interest payments for their £2.5 million stand, failed to prevent other clubs from following like lemmings the same route.

The fall-off in crowds during the 1970s has been mainly amongst working-class supporters. This is hardly surprising when most clubs seem bent on ignoring the terrace fans to concentrate on their new executive box-dwellers.

One solution is for local councils to buy grounds and then lease them back to the clubs. But from a council's point of view this makes sense only if it is also going to control the use of the ground. Football's stadiums have always been notoriously under-used. Local authority control could lead to a more rational use of their resources.

A more radical step would be to encourage multi-sport clubs on the continental model. There, successful football clubs are often part of larger organisations. The financial strength of football helps support other sports, which in turn generate additional revenue in receipts and bar and restaurant takings. The famous Spanish club Real Madrid run teams in many sports and are highly successful at basketball.

If multiple sport clubs were owned and controlled by their members then sport could be democratised. Club users could determine policy. Resources could also be exploited more efficiently. In a sport centre attached to a football club, all-weather floodlit pitches could be used by the club in the morning and open to the community in the afternoon and evening. Gymnasia, swimming baths, equipment and storage space could all be shared in this way.

Many sports in Britain have been dominated by small elites who have jealously guarded facilities and protected their own privileges. In cricket, tennis and golf working-class people are treated as interlopers and gatecrashers. The rich pickings of major occasions such as Wimbledon and the Open Championship should be used to boost sporting opportunities for ordinary people instead of maintaining the privileges of those wearing the right school tie.

The whole concept of social ownership has been seriously undermined by the negative image of the nationalised industries. While not all the hostility to nationalised industries is fair, they are for the most part large, hierarchical, inefficient bureaucracies that have done little to transform capitalism. New proposals for social ownership must be radically different – de-centralised, non-hierarchical and subject to the control of workers and users.

In the case of sport, proposals must avoid the danger of control by a faceless state. The idea should be to give power to those who work in and use sport centres, recreation grounds, swimming baths, football clubs and so on.

There are many benefits of social ownership. A more rational financial organisation would allow for a degree of cross-subsidy at present impossible. The inward-looking isolation of different sport organisations could be broken down by multi-sport clubs. A much closer relation between organisers, top performers, grassroots participants and spectators would be possible.

New structures of control would be crucial. Otherwise social ownership could generate new elite-controlled cultural bureacracy. Sport must be thoroughly democratised at all levels. Sport centres run by committees elected by workers and users of the centres could provide a basic network. (Many sport centres in the Netherlands are run on this basis.) These centres could in turn send delegates to a network of regional councils and a national council, which, unlike the present Sports Council, would then be controlled by the people it was set up to serve. Single-sport organisations could benefit similarly from a democratised structure.

In summary, a basic socialist policy for sport might contain four elements:
* An egalitarian intention. Genuine Sport For All, with positive discrimination to counter existing structures and attitudes.
* Adequate facilities and funding to make Sport For All possible.
* Social ownership of stadiums, sport centres, recreation land and

the subsidiary leisure industry.

* Democratic control of sport facilities and at all levels of sport organisations. These facilities and organisations should be controlled by those who work in and use them.

What sort of games?

The strategy outlined so far would be unlikely to succeed without broader changes in society. It would transform the organisation of sport, but not necessarily have much impact on its nature. Here changes are not a matter of legislation. The cultural patterns, habits and values embodied in particular sports will not necessarily be altered simply by new forms of ownership and control. Cultural change is a slow and complex matter.

There is no clear agreement among socialists about developing more progressive forms of sport. But there are a number of areas of potential change, where further debate could be useful. I have singled out four. First, the place, if any, of elite sport within a general Sport-For-All strategy. Second, the place, if any, of international competition between nations. Third, the whole question of competition. Fourth, the degree to which different sports should be encouraged or discouraged by differential funding.

An attack can be mounted on the whole role of elite development in sport. The pyramid form of sport organisation, in which a disproportionate amount of money, time and resources is spent nurturing small squads of top athletes for prestigious international competition can be seen as fundamentally incompatible with egalitarian principles. No special privileges should be available to those who excel. The inflated importance bestowed by the media on international competition has led to heavy spending to buy international success.

Certainly a tension exists between the demands of the elite and the needs of the grassroots. This is not confined to Britain. Communist countries like the USSR and the German Democratic Republic can claim, with rather more justification than Britain, to have developed genuine sport for all. Yet they lavish far more care on their elite athletes than does the British state. Sport in the GDR has become a highly specialised profession for which those who show prowess are systematically groomed from an early age.

The problem is one of the place of specialism. Industrialised society features a highly developed division of labour that will not simply wither and die from the first days of socialism. Socialism continues to depend on the development of special areas of knowledge, skill and expertise. A much less rigid division of labour in, say, the health service would be highly desirable. But the need for specialist doctors would remain. Are athletes so very different?

Greater participation in sport increases interest in watching skilled athletes perform. In the cinema industry many people watch films but few make them. Far more people should have the opportunity to make films but this does not mean that one day everyone will make films and no one watch them. One of the strengths of sport is that it is possible to be both a participant and a spectator. The pleasure in playing and the pleasure of watching enhance each other. And part of the pleasure of watching lies in a sense of physical skill and control that comes only with specialist expertise. Are we to give people with an aptitude for sport any less right to develop their talents than we would give to, say, musicians or electronic engineers?

I do not believe there is any easy answer to this question. International sport is so deeply embedded in the system of global relations that countries are caught up in its system of values irrespective of their own political philosophies. Elite sport at the international level has become a site for the struggle to establish national prestige. Cuba and the German Democratic Republic have both used elite sporting development to establish their legitimacy on the world stage. Sport played a significant role in the GDR's long battle to be recognised as a separate nation.

China has adopted the slogan 'Friendship Before Competition'. Yet is is beginning to dip its feet into the international pool, after many years' isolation in protest at the western inclusion of Taiwan in world events.

All these countries have had to negotiate the conflicting demands of developing an elite and extending sporting opportunity at the grassroots. Both the USSR and GDR have provided sport opportunity on a massive scale while also investing in an elite that has won substantial international success.

The problem in Britain is not so much that neither aim has been achieved. It is rather that there has been no clear public debate; no attempt to establish a precise policy about where resources should go and what the priorities should be. Britain's athletes have recently had unparalleled success and the Sports Aid Foundation has been able to raise thousands for the elite squad. Public interest has rarely been higher. Yet facilities for young athletes remain woefully inadequate. It is crude to argue that all money should be spent on grassroots sport and none on an elite level. But it is essential to determine where the balance should lie. The provision of sporting opportunity should certainly take priority over the enhancement of national prestige.

Nationalism has always been a problem for socialist analysis. National sport, as a manifestation of nationalism, presents similar problems. National sport has proved a highly successful element of bourgeois ideology. A popular cultural activity is linked to national identity, an unproblematic unity over and above political difference. It creates a largely artificial sense of national-belongingness, an imaginary coherence. It masks social divisions and antagonisms, offering a unity which we all too easily fall in with. National sport promotes that beguiling desire that England should win. We see through it and yet are part of it. National sport fosters a xenophobic attitude to foreigners – it is us against them. It helps to circulate unreal expectations of our own merits and derogatory stereotypes of everyone else.

Yet more remains to be said. The world is structured by national divisions which are not simply imaginary. But for international sport their prime significance is perhaps symbolic. So the success of the communist countries in international sport has to be explained away. It has continually to be derided, ascribed to drugs or fanaticism, or to dehumanising assembly-line methods. The massive successes of the GDR, out of all proportion to its relatively small population, make the western media particularly uneasy. The GDR women's team, which won more medals at the Montreal Olympics than all other women combined, has been described in a British paper as 'battery huns'.

The role of sport in Cuba's self-image, and in its prestige in Latin America, is important. The Cuban sporting system has won the admiration of many western coaches, notably Ron Pickering. A popular national figure like boxer Teofilio Stevenson is part of the national identity. It is dangerous to see national sport simply in a negative light. Political battles are fought with symbols. There are dangers in allowing the right to capture the power to define national identity.

Judgements about the relation between national sport and
nationalism cannot be made without considering the particular
social context. National sport plays a different role in developing
and post-colonial countries from that which it has in imperialist
powers. Similarly its role in industrialised communist countries is
rather different from its role in capitalist countries.

Take the case of Scottish football, which has a large following
among working-class Scots. The massive popularity of football in
Scotland is allied to its position as a nation within the British state.
So the annual England/Scotland game assumes a massive symbolic
importance – a contest between a subordinate nation and the
dominant state. Every second year, the soft south is invaded by the
northern hordes. The whole ritual, from the waving of yellow flags
with rampant lions and 'Remember Bannockburn' slogans to the
booing and whistling that drowns out *God Save the Queen*, is a
complex mixture of sporting fervour, expression of national identity, class consciousness and political struggle. The jeering and
booing of the national anthem has become such an embarrassment
that sport authorities have tried to defuse the hostility by using a
separate Scottish tune. But they have stuck to the traditional
Scotland the Brave, in opposition to the fans' own loudly expressed preference for *Flower of Scotland*.

International competition does not, however, necessarily mean
competition between nations though. The Olympic movement
itself, flawed from the start, and further perverted by super-power
competition and media spectacle, nevertheless had internationalist
potential.

Olympic competition was originally supposed to be between
individuals rather than nations. The organisation of teams on a
national basis was originally merely for convenience. But the
whole set of rituals – parading of teams with national flags and
medal ceremonies with flags and anthems – soon arose. The
festival became an occasion for boosting national prestige. Newspapers and broadcasting further emphasised the national element
by relaying comparative medal tables.

Yet there is another kind of symbolism in the Olympic movement to do with internationalism, coming together and peace. The
five interlocked rings on a white background that make up the
Olympic flag express the unity of the continents as opposed to
nations. The concept of the youth of all nations mingling in the

Olympic Village is internationalist in conception, even if the reality may be fraught with tension, rivalry and overcrowding. The best moments in Olympic festivals have been when the spontaneous has broken through the organised, swamping formality. At the closing ceremony of the Commonwealth Games the athletes, bored with the endless pomp and interminable speeches, broke through the cordons to dance around the track, supplanting the rigidly orchestrated television event staged for the aggrandisement of Brisbane, with something closer to the spirit of a people's festival.

One solution might be to replace formalised national sport with less formal contacts between groups and teams from different countries. There may be much to learn from the internationalism of the workers' sport movement of the inter-war years.

Competition presents another set of problems. To reject, as this book does, the argument that all competition is bad is not to accept that all forms of competition are equally acceptable. Competition can take grotesque, unpleasant and distorted forms, or friendly, co-operative and casual ones. There is also a spectrum between these extremes. Distinctions need to be made between competition between individuals, between teams, competition against records and events where individuals merely compete against their own limitations.

Many undesirable aspects of competition have already been singled out. The widespread use of drugs to improve performance is one prominent example. Anabolic steroids heighten muscular development at the long-term expense of hormonal disturbance and impairment of sexual functioning. Puberty-delaying drugs are believed to be administered to girl gymnasts. Some Finnish runners have been widely reported to use blood-doping techniques, whereby quantities of blood are removed from the body to be returned to it shortly before a major competition.

The growth of violence, be it the deliberate foul to cause injury in football and rugby, or the excess use of the whip in racing, has become a point of public concern. Rows over judging and refereeing decisions have grown to such a pitch that in sports like gymnastics, tennis and motor-racing, behind-the-scenes political battles have sometimes become more competitive than the sports themselves.

Much of the fanaticism over winning can be traced to the

enormous distinction made between winners and losers. Increasingly winning means access to great material rewards and international stardom, while losers fade quietly from the scene. Since the Moscow Olympics Coe and Ovett remain megastars. Yet how many remember Jurgen Straub, who actually finished ahead of Ovett in second place in the 1500 metres? One underlying message of the world of sport is that winning is everything and losing is nothing, even if losing is coming second.

This is the logical outcome of bourgeois culture. Winning is equated with success and happiness. Losing is equated with failure.

But competition also has a positive side. It can go hand in hand with co-operation, friendship, mutual support and genuine human aspiration. It can also be fun. Teamwork involves co-operation and all team games require co-ordination, working together alongside competition. People develop close friendships in sport even though they are rivals. The development in China of a sport system under the sign 'Friendship Before Competition' is an attempt to change the emphasis of the values inscribed in sport. Athletics events often involve strong mutual support along with rivalry, as anyone who has watched a triple jump or pole vault can tell. The finish of the first London marathon, when the two leading runners crossed the line hand in hand, was more than a bit of showbiz kitsch. It was a spontaneous response to the spirit of an event in which, for once, taking part really was more important than winning.

Even at the highest level sport can be performed with great enjoyment and mutual respect. It can also be real entertainment as opposed to mere spectacle. We need to explore ways of promoting the positive aspects of competition and diminishing the negative ones which often predominate at present.

This in turn means adopting a whole new policy towards the funding of sport. At present there are no principles as to the kinds of sport which it might be desirable to encourage. In a rationally planned society decisions have to be taken about what kind of activities to support with community resources.

Arguing for socialism means arguing that some activities are more appropriate in a humane, caring and egalitarian society than others. Funding is limited and therefore the decisions as to its allocation involve choices. These choices should be taken in the context of clear policies. Women's participation in sport is low. The tradition in state funding has been that low participation is simply an indication of low demand. If few women play sport then most do not want to play, so little attention is paid to providing for them.

Recent policy documents break with this tradition in singling out low-participation groups for attention. These proposals will remain good intentions until they are translated into action. Sports centres with proper facilities for women, full social provision for childcare, the employment of women motivators, could all increase the level of women's participation. A more consistent sport policy could go further.

Faced with demands for funding from, for example, archery, bobsleigh, curling, cycling, lacrosse and trampolining, the alternative to spreading the jam evenly, and therefore thinly, is to have a policy. Some sports are more worth of support than others. It is surely absurd that this country, which has little regular snow, and no tradition in winter sports, save that of a small stratum of the aristocracy, should spend state money in a futile attempt to gain international success in winter sports. On the other hand, it is clearly undesirable that swimming, a mass popular sport and one of the few as popular with women as with men, should still suffer from under-provision, closure of pools, reduction of opening hours and creeping privatisation.

A rational policy would also have to be imaginative. It would need to identify sports that could become popular if facilities existed. The danger at the moment is that the new high-tech sports, boosted by the entrepreneurs of the leisure industry and taken up first by the affluent young middle class, are seen uncritically. Socialists must have grave doubts about the wisdom of state funding for sports like ballooning, hang-gliding and parachuting.

There are sports that should be encouraged because of cheapness, accessibility and potential appeal. The advocates of korfball, a form of handball, point out that it is one of the few team sports in which men and women compete on equal terms. A policy committed to transforming the gender imbalance in sport participation should take this sort of claim seriously.

Participation is also low amongst ethnic minorities. Participation amongst Asians is particularly low and it is time that sport policy recognised that not everyone wants to play the games invented by

the English. When state funding goes to a whole range of oriental
martial arts it is hard to justify not funding traditional sports from
India and Pakistan.

There are pitfalls to be avoided in this approach. It would be a
naive mistake to determine funding simply on the basis of the class
image of particular sports. This book argues that sports cannot be
assigned a class-belonging like a number plate. The emergence of
tennis from middle-class suburbia does not mean that there is
something inherently middle-class about the sport itself, merely
that it was the bourgeoisie that controlled the facilities, ran the
game and determined the values and social rituals within which it
took place. This pattern was modified, but not substantially
altered, by the spread of municipal provision.

An attitude to archery, lacrosse, squash, or crown green bowls,
speedway and greyhound-racing cannot be determined simply
according to the apparent class base of the sport. More complex
questions are involved that socialists have yet to explore.

A different set of issues is raised by sports that might be pros-
cribed. All states have found the need to proscribe various sporting activities. Britain has barred not only cock-fighting and bear-
baiting, but also bull-fighting, which is permitted in Spain and
Portugal. The British Medical Association has recently launched a
campaign to outlaw boxing. It is indeed difficult to see how a sport
based centrally upon the attempt to cause more physical damage
to an opponent than he can to you can be compatible with socialist
principles. But this does not necessarily mean advocating prohibi-
tion. If boxing was banned could martial arts be left unrestricted?
The implications have yet to be explored.

Hunting, based on cruelty to animals and the private ownership
of vast tracts of land, is a far clearer case for abolition. Yet, if
hunting is banned, what justification can be found for allowing
angling? The argument that deer and foxes feel pain but not fish is
unimpressive. I would not like to find myself impaled on a giant
hook after taking a bite of cornflakes. I see no reason why fish
should feel differently. We are cruel to a whole range of animals in
the name of agriculture. But this is no reason why we should claim
a licence for further cruelty in the name of sport. It seems to me an
entirely inadequate defence of both boxing and fishing to
say that they have a large working-class following. There is a
great danger of hypocrisy if the logic of socialist principles

is not followed through to its inevitable conclusion.

A radical approach to policy formation should also consider the form of sport events. One implication of the critique of elite sport and of the separation of different sports is that it would make sense to switch from major single-sport events to multi-sport, multi-ability people's festivals. There is a lot of scope for the promotion of such events by local councils.

All the questions raised need further exploration. If a distinct socialist approach is to emerge, the issues of elite sport, national-ism and internationalism, forms of competition and types of sport to encourage will need discussion. The need is not for glib over-simple policies but for a continuing debate that takes the real complexities on board.

A culture of sport

England played an influential part in the formation of many sports. Its forms of organisation have been copied all over the world. Varied and rich cultures surround different sports. But there is little public discussion of sport and society. This country has produced no reflective philosophy of sport. Everything about sporting activity is taken for granted.

The media report sport with great professional skill but discuss it with a crass lack of seriousness. Newspapers relay results efficient-ly and delight in trivial controversy, but are timid and uninforma-tive about the organisation of sport. Television sport takes up as much as one-sixth of air time and is for the vast majority of the population the public face of sport. The technical sophistication of living colour and slow-motion replay is remarkable. So is its failure to produce informative sport journalism.

Britain has no weekly sports newspaper, no equivalent to the French journal *L'Equipe*. Since the demise of *Sportsworld* the only monthly magazines covering a range of sports are house journals like *Sport and Leisure* (the Sports Council) and *Action* (the Physical Education Association). Most sports publications are glossy magazines aimed at single sports.

They are heavily constrained by the advertising imperative. So up-market sports, which appeal to affluent consumers, are best served. Water sport, motor sport, golf and tennis, are covered by a wide range of titles.

The journals that exploit the new boom in popular running all emphasise equipment – the best shoes, track suits and so on – in both articles and adverts. Many sports journals owe their success to the growth of spending on leisure and sport goods.

There is no place in which a dialogue between socialists interested in sport and sports people with a socialist outlook might develop. If progress towards the sort of transformations suggested in this book is to be made, then a site needs to be found to develop the discussion.

For sport to develop it must be forced out of its self-imposed ghetto. Sport is not separate from social life as a whole, nor is it separate from cultural life. It is not a natural activity which cannot be changed and need not be discussed.

There is scope for a new form of local centre. It could contain library facilities, exhibition space, meeting space, workshops with community-owned tools and equipment, cafés, nursery and laundry facilities and sport provision. Such centres, democratically run, could provide an alternative to privatised use of leisure time, and a way of integrating sport into social life generally.

If a people's culture of sport is to emerge it needs to be built from below. It must not be based on a new level of cultural bureaucracy. Cuba has over 50,000 people actively involved in voluntary sport councils. These people are not simply functionaries who do the leg-work. They do not just organise events. They also work in factories, farms and offices to make sport popular. They produce media material – film and television items, posters and press reports. They are not officials but motivators. Their activity is given a framework by the socialist organisation of the society.

Sport policy in this country has recently begun to place more emphasis on the role of motivator. But motivation will succeed fully only if it is allied with adequate provision and an overall strategy for making sport an integrated part of full human development.

In short, real change in the nature of sport depends on a broader socialist transformation. But that does not mean that developments in sport provision should be ignored. On the contrary, any chance of developing multi-activity local centres and promoting genuine people's festivals should be pursued.

The Regional Recreation Strategy of the Greater London and South-East Council for Sport and Recreation contains a number of outline plans for new facilities. Two are of great interest: the possible redevelopment of Battersea Power Station and Alexandra Palace as sport and community centres. In the present economic climate these plans are unlikely to gain state support. If they did, they could still become rather over-priced, semi-privatised leisure centres for the affluent.

But, properly funded and democratically controlled, they could become pioneering examples of a new form of community centre – a people's palace. There are many problems to be overcome, problems that apply to the whole concept of community centres. But it is an idea worth fighting for.

Fighting cuts and privatisation is not enough. We need a positive alternative to struggle for. This should not be a return to the bureaucratised drabness of the municipal tradition. It should re-vitalise people's relation to their facilities.

Hopefully the need to argue for socialist policies in an arena that reaches those involved in sport is obvious. The underlying rationale of this series of books is the need to make socialist ideas popular. We cannot afford to talk only to the converted.

A Guide to Reading

There are countless thousands of books about sport, the great majority of which are biographies of great names, memories of great moments or coaching manuals. Some of these are of great merit, many others are hastily produced ghost-written attempts to cash in on fame. To keep this guide short I have concentrated on three areas of specific interest to readers of this book: socialist accounts of sport, histories and information about policy.

There are three socialist accounts of particular interest. *Sport, a Prison of Measured Time* by Jean-Marie Brohm (Inklinks 1978) is the most elaborate critique of the whole institution of sport as such to appear in book form to date. *Sport, Culture and Ideology*, edited by Jenny Hargreaves (Routledge and Kegan Paul 1982), is an excellent collection, with contributions on youth culture, football hooliganism, women and sport, sport in the Soviet Union, apartheid, drugs and television sport. *Beyond a Boundary* by West Indian marxist C. L. R. James (Stanley Paul 1963) is a remarkable book, which weaves together autobiography, cricket, politics, literature and art and asks, 'What do they know of cricket, who only cricket know?' Essential reading for anyone interested in sport.

There are several books that develop critiques of sport. *Rip Off the Big Game* by Paul Hoch (New York: Anchor 1972), *Football Mania* by Gerhard Vinnai (Ocean 1973), *From Ritual to Record* by Allen Guttman (New York: Columbia University Press 1978) and *The Name of the Game* by Fred Inglis (Heinemann 1977) are the most relevant to Chapter Two.

There are a number of accounts of the struggle against apartheid in sport. *The South African Game* by Robert Archer and Antone

Bouillon (Zed Press 1982) has a detailed explanation of the South African sport system. *Apartheid, the Real Hurdle* by Sam Ramsamy of SANROC (International Defence and Aid Fund for South Africa 1982) outlines the political struggle to isolate South African sport and South African attempts to undermine the boycott. *Don't Play with Apartheid* by Peter Hain (Allen and Unwin 1970) relates the story of the highly successful campaign to stop the 1970 cricket tour by South Africa.

The recent rise of black people in British sport has been documented in *Black Sportsmen* by Ernest Cashmore (Routledge and Kegan Paul 1982). The book contains many interesting interviews but concentrates, without offering any reason, almost exclusively on men.

The history of sport is poorly documented. Most general histories tend to ignore sport, while most histories of sport are little more than reminiscences of great occasions and top stars of the past. The books listed here are an exception and consequently a major source for anyone interested in the development of sport and leisure. *Sport and Society, from Elizabeth to Anne* by Dennis Brailsford (Routledge and Kegan Paul 1969), *Popular Recreations in English Society 1700–1850* by Robert Malcolmson (Cambridge University Press 1973) and *Leisure in the Industrial Revolution* by Hugh Cunningham (Croom Helm 1980) are all useful accounts of the development of sport before its reorganisation in the second half of the nineteenth century. The rise of public school sport is examined in *Athleticism in the Victorian and Edwardian Public School* by J. A. Mangan (Cambridge University Press 1981). *Physical Education in England since 1800* by Peter McIntosh (Bell and Hyman 1968) traces the emergence of distinctive ways in which sport and physical activity have been handled in schools. Brian Dobbs's *Edwardians at Play 1890–1914* (Pelham 1973) is a valuable account of the place of sport in this pre-war period. For a general history covering the whole period to the present day, *This Sporting Land* by John Ford (New English Library/Thames 1977) makes a useful introduction.

Only a few histories of specific sports place events in any kind of social context. Among the more useful are *English Cricket* by Christopher Brookes (Weidenfeld and Nicolson 1978), *The People's Game* by James Walvin (Allen Lane 1975), *Association Football and English Society 1863–1915* by Tony Mason

(Harvester 1980), *Golf in Britain* by Geoffrey Cousins (Routledge and Kegan Paul 1975), *The Official Centenary History of the AAA* by Peter Lovesey (Guinness Superlatives 1979) and *The Complete Book of Athletics* by Tom McNab (Ward Lock 1980).

Only a Game by Eamon Dunphy (Kestrel 1976) is a remarkable diary of a football season, far more revealing about the game than sport autobiographies. As an antidote to the perennial hysteria over 'football hooliganism', *Football Hooliganism: The Wider Context*, a collection of pieces edited by Roger Ingham (Inter-Action Inprint 1978), is a source of alternative explanations. There is interesting material on the historical origins of British football in *The Sociology of Sport*, edited by Eric Dunning (Cass 1976).

So far there is a regrettable absence of book-length accounts of women and sport in this country, although there are articles and papers. *Sport, Culture and Ideology* (already listed) contains some material on women, sport and leisure. Margaret Talbot's review paper *Women and Leisure* (Sports Council/SSRC 1980) has references in the broader area of leisure. Historical sources include *The Nineteenth-Century Woman, Her Cultural and Physical World* by Sara Delamont and Lorna Duffin (Croom Helm 1978), *Hidden from History* by Sheila Rowbotham (Pluto 1973) and *English Costumes for Sports and Outdoor Recreations* by P. Cunnington and A. Mansfield (Adam and Charles Black 1969). *Catching Up the Men* by K.F. Dyer (Junction 1982) contains a detailed examination of the narrowing performance gap betwen women and men in top sport. There is a lot of material about women and sport in America, much of it in the tradition of functional sociology. One of the better books is *Women and Sport, from Myth to Reality* by Carole Oglesby (Philadelphia: Lea and Febiger 1978).

More information about the sport system in other countries is available mainly in article form, but two books worth examination are *Sport under Communism*, edited by James Riordan (Hurst 1978) and Don Anthony's *A Strategy for British Sport* (Hurst 1980). James Riordan has also written extensively about sport in the Soviet Union, in *Sport in Soviet Society* (Cambridge University Press 1977) and *Soviet Sport* (Blackwell 1980).

Football is the only sport with a developed form of trade union and a history of organised struggles over pay and conditions. For information about this, try *Soccer Rebel* by Jimmy Guthrie (Davis

Foster 1976), *Striking for Soccer* by Jimmy Hill (Peter Davies 1961), *On the Spot* by Derek Dougan and Percy M. Young (Stanley Paul 1975), *Hardaker of the League* by Alan Hardaker (Pelham 1977), *The Football Revolution* by George W. Keeton (David and Charles 1977) and the *Chester Report on Football* (DES 1968). The brief account of workers' sport organisations between the wars offered in this book is based upon two articles in *Journal of Contemporary History*, vol. 13 no. 2, April 1978.

Despite the prominence of television sport there is as yet no comprehensive study in book form. Football coverage is discussed in *Football on Television*, edited by Edward Buscombe (British Film Institute 1975) and there is a paper on *Television Coverage of Sport* by Roy Peters (available from Centre for Contemporary Cultural Studies, University of Birmingham 1975). Otherwise the main accounts are in biographical form, perhaps the most interesting being *Cue Frank* by Frank Bough (Macdonald Futura 1980). Now this book is finished I hope to write up my own extensive research into television sport.

There are two books of relevance to the discussion of sport policy, the official history of the CCPR, *Service to Sport*, by H. Justin Evans (Pelham 1974) and Don Anthony's *A Strategy for British Sport* (already listed). Otherwise information about policy is largely in the form of official reports, documents and research papers. In particular anyone interested in sport policy ought to look at *Sport in the Community: The Next Ten Years*, the current Sports Council strategical plan. Each regional Sports Council has also recently published a *Regional Recreation Strategy*. The Sports Council and the Social Science Research Council have jointly published a range of research papers, including material on women, youth, ethnic and elderly leisure patterns and private and state leisure organisation. A complete list of reports, documents and leaflets published or distributed by the Sports Council is available from the Publications Department, The Sports Council, 16 Upper Woburn Place, London WC1H OQP.